# PREDICTIVE SOCIAL MEDIA

## A GUIDE TO MASTERING CORE VALUES, RELATIONSHIPS, AND A DISRUPTIVE SYSTEM THAT IS CHANGING THE WORLD OF BUSINESS

## JIM LUPKIN

*for you, the reader—*
*those who want to live an extraordinary personal*
*and business life*
*by harnessing the power of social media*

SPOV Publishing

spovpublishing.com

Events and conversations in this book come from the author's recollections. As such, they are not intended to read as word-for-word transcripts but retold in a way to evoke meaning. In all cases, the author has attempted to honor the essence of dialog and happenings. Some names and identifying details have been changed to protect the privacy of individuals.

Lupkin, Jim,

Predictive Social Media: A Guide to Mastering Core Values, Relationships, and a Disruptive System That Is Changing the World of Business / by Jim Lupkin.—1st ed.

ISBN: 978-1-7370368-0-7 (ebook)

ISBN: 978-1-7370368-1-4 (pbk)

1. Business Communication 2. E-Commerce – Small Business 3. Entrepreneurship

Cover ©2021 by Code Cherry Designs

Interior design and layout by Christina Hovland

Edited by L.A. Mitchell

For information regarding speaking engagements, to book an event, or to contact Jim for social media expertise or help in applying Predictive Social Media for your business, visit jimlupkin.com.

# CONTENTS

# INTRODUCTION

**THE SEVEN CS OF THE PREDICTIVE SOCIAL MEDIA SYSTEM**

COMMUNICATION

CAPABILITIES

CONNECTION

CONTRIBUTION

COMPLIANCE

COMMUNITY

CONVERSATION

I DIDN'T START WITH 7CS—pillars upon which my entire system stood. For many years, I didn't know what I had *was* a system. I simply entered into relationships online with others who wanted to purchase my products or services, and I taught businesses how to do the same.

Eventually, after many trials and no small amount of errors, results validated everything I believed about social media.

Words I'd used frequently in my consults began to congregate around one alphabet letter—C—and the culmination of those words and ideas and truths formed the foundation of this book.

A quick look at the Cs that make up my Predictive Social Media system:

*Contribution* – embracing your values and overcoming personal development hurdles to ensure that social media interactions become lasting and fruitful relationships.

*Capabilities* – mastering the basics of the social media platforms of your choice so that you optimize your relationship-building efforts.

*Compliance* – understanding the legalities and limitations of your business via social media interactions.

*Conversation* – the ability to have authentic and robust interactions about your personal and business life with your social media friends.

*Community* – the place on social media where people can hear from others who love your product or service.

*Connection* – accessing an endless supply of potential customers and people who will refer your business to others while building real relationships.

*Communication* – staying in touch the right way to build enduring relationships for your business to thrive.

Will there be other Cs to come? Probably. Like you, I continue to be molded by my experiences. Someone suggested *coffee* and *chocolate* should be involved because it all sounds so formidable.

But I have a secret for you.

You're already doing some of the things in the Cs. The hill to climb isn't as steep as you might think. Reframing your mindset and daily tweaks to your social media activity will take you far.

And one of the—dare I say—*magical* parts of the 7Cs is the energy it takes on when you're not on social media. Values and relationships and predictive outcomes happen behind the scenes, while you retain ultimate control over how much social media to allow into your day.

**The 7Cs work in unison.** If you allow one or two Cs to slide away or believe some components are not as integral as others, you won't realize the system's full benefit. A rainbow has seven colors. Without some of the colors, the effect wouldn't be as spectacular. Embrace all the Cs. Seek out their interconnectedness. Master that blend of core values, relationships, and systems, and you'll experience swift and life-altering success.

# CHAPTER ONE

## Values, Relationships, and Systems

PREDICTIVE SOCIAL MEDIA.

Sounds a little unrealistic, doesn't it? After all, humans are wildly unpredictable creatures with agendas and baggage and fears that guide behaviors. That hasn't stopped business from trying to predict the thoughts and actions of consumers since paper advertising and radio ads reached people at their most vulnerable—in their houses, on their commutes, in all the personal spaces people move and gather.

And now, social media.

For two hours and twenty-five minutes, on average, every day, people immerse themselves in a virtual world of entertainment with little mental pushback.[1] Consider the endorphins that rush fans of major league sports championships each year as million-dollar ads run. Now imagine that captive audience, ten-fold.

That's social media.

Yet, in this newest and most energized business frontier the world has ever known, no one has been able to successfully predict outcomes for word of mouth, for customer referrals, for friends telling friends on social media.

Until now.

Before social media, word of mouth was unpredictable. Typically, businesses launched to great fanfare and parties. Friends celebrated with friends inside a dedicated community of people who shared an emotional investment in the business. Then, as soon as the business became successful enough to have a marketing budget, these same businesses abandoned their customer referral strategy and sank money into things that had better tracking metrics—like internet advertising, pay-per-click on Google and other search engines, and offline strategies.

Well-worn marketing paths have their time and place. They work. But what happened to the fanfare and parties? What happened to friends telling friends and that contagious enthusiasm that seemed powerful enough to will a business to succeed? Where did the endorphins go?

That emotional investment still exists. It happens every minute, every post, every day on countless platforms. And yet, businesses cannot linger in that dynamic space because numbers don't attach to a feeling.

Or do they?

If you're holding this book or if my voice is reaching your ears, you've likely been tasked with conquering this frontier. You're a pilot inside a cockpit of expectations placed upon you by your corporation, your small business, or that voice inside you as an independent contractor or brand. Maybe your goal isn't business. Finding love, finding purpose—heck, even finding a kidney—counts (more about that later).

If you love social media, welcome. I love it too. Despite its sometimes-controversial reputation, social media has the capacity to be the greatest force for good that humanity has ever known. If you dislike social media, sit beside me. The future is bright.

In this cockpit is a metaphorical series of levers and buttons and tabs and dials that represent all the actions you can take on any social media platform on any given day. Using one dial correctly does not guarantee you'll know anything about the lever beside it. Pulling, pushing, sliding, and turning produces outcomes that seem random, at best.

**What if there was a way to know with absolute certainty which motions, in order, for a specified duration, yielded maximum results? All reasons to look elsewhere for a word-of-mouth social media strategy would be eliminated.** Further, what if this system was a force for good and lifted people in the process?

Too good to be true? With the right combination of value-based entrepreneurial thinking, relationship-building mindset, personal growth that silences the obstacles between our ears, and actions that deliver predictive results, the seemingly ideal becomes real for your business or brand.

Right now, I want to deliver to you something that sets me apart from social media experts, trainers, coaches, consultants, public relations firms, and advertising companies. I am none of those. I am a systems architect. I look at a problem and ask, *What is the proper sequence, timing, and process to give me a predictive result so I don't have that problem anymore?*

The predictive part of my system leans into basic algebra. What better way to explore guaranteed outcomes than a formula? The formula presented below represents brand advocates.

Brand advocates are customers or employees of a company who actively go out into the world and turn social media's attention onto a product or service. Think third-party cheerleaders who use their established social media to share their love of your business. Anyone who uses Predictive Social Media on a daily basis is a brand advocate.

Get ready to know the how, when, and why inside your cockpit of expectations. Your social media world will never be the same.

# THE FORMULA

To best understand the formula's breakdown, a few terms:

- **Brand Advocate:** Anyone actively going out and implementing this system on behalf of a company, small business, brand, or individual business. Someday, artificial intelligence may master this, but for now, a brand advocate is a human being. I used the term *brand advocate* to represent an individual who shares a product or service. Different industries may use different terms than those presented in this book. For clarity, I'll stick to the term brand advocate.
- **Total Brand Advocates/Active Base:** The total number of people actively applying this system on behalf of a company, small business, brand, or individual business. This variable can represent six employees running a food truck or thousands of distributors in a global company. Note, the emphasis is on active.
- **The 80/20 Rule (also known as the Pareto Principle):** Named after an Italian economist, Vilfredo Pareto, who, in 1848, first noticed the outcome pattern with pea pods in his garden and later applied this philosophy to many aspects of life. This principle is widely researched and accepted as a universal truth: 80% of the results will come from only 20% of the action.

Some people won't carry out the system exactly the way I advise, for whatever reason. The Pareto Principle tells us that at least 20% of the people will engage with the system the right way.

The system gets results, but we must account for human behavior.

# BRAND ADVOCATE FORMULA

$$(((((\text{total brand advocates}) \times 20\%) \times \text{people per day}) \times \text{days}) \text{ divide by } 5) \times 20\%$$

|           A           |      B      | C | D |

## SECTION A:

**(Total brand advocates) x .20)**
Applying the 80/20 rule, we assume that .20 (or 20%) of the total brand advocates will do the majority of the action. Out of six food truck employees, one will implement the system. Out of 100 brand advocates, twenty will actively apply the system.

## SECTION B:

**x people per day x days**
Explored further in the Conversation chapter, this part of the formula addresses the number of invitations extended by individual brand advocates each day for a specific unit of days set forth by the goals of the company, small business, brand, or individual business. If a brand advocate reaches out to 10 people per day for 90 days, the reach of that one brand advocate during that time is 900 people. Be sure to only count working days. Even the most dedicated people deserve recharge days.

## SECTION C:

**Divide by 5**
If you do my system correctly, in its entirety, 1 out of every 5 will become a customer, a customer referrer, or a brand advocate to promote your business. This is known as process conversion.

Take a minute to digest.

# *One* out of *five*.

Many companies don't know their process conversion ratio because nothing in the world of business or advertising—online or offline—gives such accurate predictability. If companies are aware of their numbers, if they already believe they are experiencing healthy, predictive outcomes, they're likely getting a process conversion of—at best—1 out of 20.

A system is different. A system delivers efficiency. Predictive Social Media secures one out of five.

This ratio comes from what I have been able to achieve in more than twenty-five years of applying this system over the evolution of social media. My system will not merely create incremental success for you; Predictive Social Media is a disruptor. If you follow this system, you *will* see 1 out of 5 results.

SECTION D:

**x .20**
Back to the Pareto Principle. Some people—about 20%—will buy or act right away. The rest of them may purchase in 30 days or 45 days, after they think on it or ask a trusted friend for an opinion. It's a trickle effect. Section D of the formula represents the percentage of people who will act right away, without delay.

As you can see, there's plenty of room built into the formula for the results to be even greater. The formula represents baseline results and is the most foundational mathematical principle in Predictive Social Media. Enhanced versions of the formula incorporate factors such as attrition rates in the six-month drop off when most brand advocates tend to leave their position because they've hit income goals, number of total customers, and customer attrition rates, and are available through Predictive Social Media's online resources.

## PREDICTIVE SOCIAL MEDIA

Business has been chasing the fantasy of Predictive Social Media since the advent of internet relay chats (IRCs) and the first widely recognized social media site, Six Degrees, launched in 1997. To take a finite quantity of a business' marketing budget and inject it into the unknown was a frightening, albeit exciting, prospect.

I've been chasing that fantasy longer.

As a young man, my business empire rested on a flame-broiled, fast food burger. An assembly line of burgers, actually—each one emblazoned with fake marks so that customers thought the frozen meat had made an authentic connection with a grill. A manager in a paper hat told me I wasn't smart enough to run the drive-thru window. By eighteen, I was an entrepreneur, a businessman, the CEO of my enterprise. Instead of Friday Night Lights, I made Friday night cold-calls out of the phone book and exhausted my mom's network of friends. I often approached people who pumped gas with vacant stares, shook hands, and asked them if they wanted more money in their pockets by being a brand advocate for my business because fuel prices were on the rise. Most of the time, I was obnoxious in that rare, perfect storm of naiveté and optimism and youth.

It was small-town Pennsylvania, 1997. I took the fast-food job to know at least one meal a day was guaranteed, to have access to disposable food at shift's end so my mom didn't have to ration canned meat and saltines. I wasn't above flipping burgers or draining oil from fry vats, but I lacked the ability to feel complacent.

On one memorable dumpster haul, a woman in a BMW 5 series idled in the drive-thru lane. Despite the frigid temperatures, despite her third position in the queue, her window remained down. Jazz music flurried from her stereo. Ebony hair twisted neatly atop her crown. Shiny rings adorned nearly every tapping finger on her steering wheel. We made eye contact.

She smiled. "Hey, son. Keep up the good work."

Her jubilant fingertips continued to play the steering wheel in time to the melody as if she was responsible for the brassy trumpet notes lifting into the night. The movement, the lightness in her tone, radiated warmth. I set the trash bags on the ground at my feet.

"Miles Davis?" I asked.

"Coltrane. But I'm impressed. Someone's done right by you." Her voice lingered on syllables the way the brass instrument improvised space inside the tune.

"My mom loves all types of music."

The woman nodded her head. Cars advanced ahead of her. She inched her luxury car forward, clearing a path to the dumpster.

I didn't move. The familiar stirring in my gut at first contact edged me closer to courage. She had her act together. I wanted the same.

"I have a business proposition for you," I said. "Ten minutes. All I need to change your life."

She propped the sleeve of her fancy coat on the door. "That so?"

I gave her my hyper-speed pitch, three lines, maybe four, before I added, "I'm just working here until I build my empire."

Her laughter rose above the idling engines.

I handed her a business card from my uniform pocket then remembered my filthy hands, my job, my place. I apologized.

"I live two hours from here, son. In Philly."

"I'll drive to you."

"I'll just bet you would."

My manager's voice edged closer, through the kitchen's side door. I picked up the trash bags and completed my haul to the dumpster. On my way back inside, the woman waved.

The next day, a familiar, slow-talking voice over the phone said, "Is this the young man who's going to change my life?"

Not a jazz number goes by that I don't remember that encounter. The next day, I made the two-hour drive and signed her and a few of her friends to my telecommunication service. For a time, I believed success was mine—my confidence, my courage. The perfect storm of naiveté and optimism and youth. Years later, I learned that I owed my success to Miles Davis.

Talking to a stranger in a drive-thru is networking. Talking to a stranger in a drive-thru about Miles Davis then staying in touch on a social networking site is social media. The internet is a potent business tool, unprecedented in reach and possibility, but it can also be a lonely, fruitless place without authentic connection.

Social media today is the basis of most relationships. It's how friends stay connected with each other and meet new friends. We all want to be part of something bigger than ourselves. We want to connect and communicate with like-minded people. We want to be part of a group of friends that know us, and we want to trust the people we have allowed into our circle. Effective social media is reaching out to make new connections online, having great conversations, continuing the valuable communication over time, and building trusted relationships with the community you have inspired.

It took me years of achievements and failures to identify three elements that make up the ideal social media system. **Core values and relationships** kickstart the system and prepare you for the basic **algebra** that incorporates timing, sequence, and process. Like tripod legs that hold a perfectly focused lens, one or two elements do not work without all three.

Core values focus inward. You cannot be all the things you need to be uniquely you on social media without understanding your guiding principles and fundamental beliefs.

Relationships focus outward. Building healthy relationships online does not come naturally to most people, me included. The shrapnel of our past failed associations often gets in the way.

Core values and relationships comprise the Contribution portion of the Predictive Social Media system.

The system's remaining six components—together with Contribution, known as the 7Cs—are far more than a tool. It's an entire system, backed by science, that works in beautiful harmony to achieve the outcome you set forth.

## CORE VALUES

At one time, I believed my core values were travel and time freedom. I'd found the words on a website and thought they fit. After all, how many 20-something entrepreneurs jet off to India for three months to chase down dreams? And who doesn't love a day that stretches into 32 hours with less of them tangled in work?

Imagine that—I had based the guiding principles of my life on a Google search. They are values, but they don't go deep enough. We're talking soul-level, heart-level stuff.

Core.

Then I met Sandra Harry and Kathy Lawson. Thirty-five years ago, they were some of the first people trained by Dr. Mikel J. Harry to become black belts in Six Sigma. Both women were instrumental in conceptualizing Six Sigma's fourth generation, the portion of the system that reaches beyond business into life. Their understanding of core values was deep. Mariana-Trench deep.

The onion method of peeling back layers is not new to business, but it certainly applies here. Sandra and Kathy pressed me to ask myself *Why travel? Why time freedom?* Of those answers, I asked why, again and again, at a depth that brought me close to hard truths and not a little discomfort, until I had distilled my answers to what truly brought me joy.

Joy inside the most mundane of tasks. Joy at the cellular level while getting out of bed each morning. Joy that kept me inside a pocket of positivity and momentum.

That joy is your core values.

Your core values can be a noun, a verb, a phrase you scribbled on a fast-food napkin, a quote that hits you in the feels, or any word or combination of words that elicits goosebumps, that allows you to self-indulge—for that small space of time—and just be, authentically *you*.

One of mine is *glow*. More about that later.

Assemble five of them and you're on your way to a heart-centered, life-altering business journey.

## RELATIONSHIPS

Eighteen years ago, a friend who has been recognized as one of the most successful individuals in the direct sales industry told me, "When the masses are able to build real relationships online in the way that they can build them offline and a company embraces it entirely, that company will become the largest direct sales company in history—and maybe the largest company in all of business."

Nearly everyone in business recognizes the importance of relationships. If you project yourself into the world in a manner that turns people away, your business takes on that toxicity. This base-level understanding, however, turns into base-level results. To truly understand the fundamentals of relationships within my system, an almost-seismic shift in philosophy is necessary.

> It's *not* about building a relationship *so that* a person will do business with you.
>
> It's about building a relationship *even if* that person will *never* do business with you.

Predictive Social Media puts friendship ahead of business. Always.

## SYSTEM

Many who wish to streamline various aspects of business *say* they have a system.

Most don't.

Baseline definitions of timing, sequence, and process clarify the true nature of a system.

Timing is the ability to select a precise moment to do something for optimum effect. For example, the Conversation portion of my system addresses when you should follow up with people privately who have expressed interest in your product or service.

Sequence is a set of related events or movements that follow each other in a particular order. Without a doubt, sequence is the portion of the system that generates the most questions. The system teaches you *in what order* you should pull the levers of your social media for optimum results.

Process is a series of steps taken in order to achieve an end. The 7Cs of my social media system represent an entire process, but you'll find a process inside each component, as well.

**True systems contain timing, sequence, and process.** When I hear the latest buzz method or trick in business, I investigate further.

- Is the method complete? Can I identify the timing, sequence and process that leads to a predictive result?
- Can the method be easily handed off to another individual, or do I need to work with someone in order to find success? Predictive Social Media works independent of any one person. Once you learn the system, the outcome is in your hands.
- Can I understand the method and implement it with minimal Q&A? Systems are simple to understand because systems read like map instructions: do this, do that, get this. Straight forward.
- If implemented exactly, will I achieve the predicted outcome? After the correct sequence, timing, and process is applied, does it deliver the same predictive result?

If the answer to any of the above questions is no, the method isn't a system. It's a tool.

Tools make life easier and businesses better. Tools conquer narrow goals with grand efficiency. What's more effective than tools? A system.

A friend named Jerry, who was having trouble deciphering between a tool and system, once told me his epiphany of understanding.

"If I do what Jim says, the correct timing, sequence, and process, and I don't judge, I just do it, then the result is predictive."

Not only did I know this was the moment Jerry had internalized this key difference, he gifted me the perfect word for my system that had eluded me: predictive.

Thanks, Jerry.

Systems are beautiful. That one person can develop a process of timing and sequence such that anyone can apply it and realize the same results is nothing short of miraculous to me. A little like the attention my system received from Six Sigma.

## SIX SIGMA

In the 1980s, Dr. Mikel J. Harry was an engineer at Motorola. The company was on the verge of bankruptcy because they sold pagers that did not work. Along with his co-engineer and friend, Bill Smith, Harry developed a step-by-step system that increased efficiency on the manufacturing floor.

In general terms, the methodology involved identifying a problem, collecting data surrounding the process where the problem occurs, developing potential solutions driven by the data, testing those potential solutions, creating a system around the best solution, and measuring results as needed. It wasn't hard to see the scientific method's influence in what Harry and Smith developed. What they did next changed the course of Motorola, and business as we know it today, forever.

Not content to rest on their winning strategy, they improved the system and applied it to employees, teams, and management. Essentially, they created a sustainable business strategy still in use today by 87% of Fortune 100 companies, 66% of Fortune 500 companies in the US, and many global corporations around the world.

Why do companies like Amazon, American Express, 3M, Bank of America, Honda, and Toshiba implement Six Sigma today? Because it works. Identifying and applying the right sequence, timing, and process is as much of an art as there will ever be in business. When backed by math and science-based truths, the results are atomic.

In truth, only 5% of the business world has truly touched the depth and power of this methodology. Six Sigma continues to discover applications beyond the business world. People use Six Sigma methodologies to lose weight, find love, and live their true calling. The possibilities are staggering.

Dr. Mikel J. Harry opened my eyes to the importance of sequence, timing, and process. Beyond that, his friendship transformed my life.

When I developed my Predictive Social Media system, I applied Six Sigma's philosophy for developing simple systems that yielded maximum success. **Dr. Mikel was impressed at how my system produced the caliber of results the world had come to expect with his world-renowned Six Sigma. To Dr. Mikel, and many others, my system is Six Sigma for social media.**

But don't take my word for it. Dr. Mikel J. Harry, in his words:

---

Some of you might recognize my name as being associated with Six Sigma, a business management system designed to improve the profitability of corporations. As a matter of fact, we deployed Six Sigma throughout Allied Signal, Honeywell, GE, Ford, and DuPont corporations, just to name a few, with unbelievable success. The system encouraged business to run more effectively and efficiently. Put simply, Six Sigma reshaped the way industry executes its work on a daily basis.

To do that, we didn't really invent anything. With Six Sigma, we built on the work of others and innovated the proper sequence, timing, and process—essentially the same inspired philosophy that Jim Lupkin has embraced his entire professional career. He hasn't invented anything, but his innovation is far-reaching. His vision and principles have phenomenal implications.

As with Six Sigma, Jim understands the best way to craft those nuances in an orderly, progressive, and meaningful way so that the social part of your business has maximum impact.

Social media. In a nutshell, what is it? It's about people coming together to build on a product or service: the features, the benefits, the merits, the value associated with that product or services.

Jim Lupkin is an amazing man. He's a dear friend of mine and colleague, whom I consider an absolute genius in the field of social media. Get into his innovation, learn all you can about it, and you'll find you have the same reaction as me: Whoa! I wish this had been around when I started Six Sigma thirty years ago. Would have made my life a lot easier.

Just as with Six Sigma, generating breakthrough faster, quicker, more efficiently, and more effectively than would otherwise be possible is only the beginning of what you can accomplish. With Jim's system, you're well on your way.

Dr. Mikel J. Harry
Co-Creator/Six Sigma
March 2017

Sadly, my good friend passed away a few months after he wrote these words. I miss my chats with him and how he would make me think in new ways. I liken our interactions to a fish, swimming along in a current, oblivious to a human observing the activity from above and seeing the greater picture. I was the fish; Mikel always saw the world in ways I never imagined. He never hesitated to share his view. I will forever remain in a place of gratitude for our friendship.

Now that you understand the magnitude of Six Sigma, entertaining other social media systems seems hollow. What I share with you in these pages will change your outlook—in business and, perhaps, in life. Even if you only ever implement what you read in this book, you will find success. As with Six Sigma, the scope of Predictive Social Media cannot possibly be contained between these two covers.

Take this journey with me, discover your business within my system, and stay with me beyond the final sentence.

## FINDING YOURSELF IN PREDICTIVE SOCIAL MEDIA

No matter where your entrepreneurial spirit takes you, there is a place for you in the system.

People see themselves, and their businesses, through different lenses. Some see themselves as independent contractors because they receive a 1099 tax form at the end of the year. A small, startup business might view another more established startup as a company. I encourage you to discover the term attached to your unique business so that in subsequent chapters, when the system gets into specifics, you'll feel confident in the mindset and actions that will most benefit your situation.

Broader terms of **entrepreneurs** and **businesses** will be used interchangeably. Brand advocates, independent contractors, small businesses, brands, and companies are grouped under these terms.

## BRANDS

Brands are a special term in Predictive Social Media. Brands function like small businesses but are unique in that they build up a name, like an influencer, not a product or service. Let's say you ran a successful motor racing business for twenty years, rebuilding cars back to their former glory. You became a bit of a local celebrity, sold t-shirts, sponsored concerts, and eventually sold your small business to go on a publicity tour and share with other auto shops how to tap into that lifestyle market in their local market. Now, you're a brand. Your name is paramount to whatever business you may have had in the past.

## BRAND ADVOCATES

The success of Predictive Social Media rests on brand advocates. If you think the term doesn't apply to your business, think again.

The term *brand advocate* applies to *all* sizes of businesses in the following ways:

- **For independent contractors and influencers**, you are your own brand advocate, operating without a team.
- **For small businesses** who may not want to flesh out a deliberate brand advocate program, your small group of employees or sales team are your brand advocates.
- **For large companies and corporations**, brand advocates are an enhanced, aspirational version of what we know today as an affiliate program. These are the people who share your

company's products and want to earn a commission for going out and telling their friends. Because your company's affiliate program is already built on people who are tech savvy, likely your marketing team and energized customers who are motivated to share your product or service, brand advocates have the potential to catapult your company's success.

**The minute you start applying the Predictive Social Media system, you become a brand advocate. The term** *brand advocate* **applies to every individual selling a product or service using Predictive Social Media.** Today's brand advocates are known by many names—influencers, affiliates, consultants, distributors. In an ideal world of business, these terms would converge under one, united descriptor because they all fill the same role.

Businesses who have brand advocate programs enjoy greater brand awareness, higher sales, increased website traffic, better quality leads, enhanced employer ratings, and larger pools of stellar talent. Brand advocates also enjoy the tremendous freedom of a remote-work lifestyle.

The year 2020 has proven itself a tipping point in work expectations and structure. The coronavirus pandemic and subsequent quarantines and social distancing mandates worldwide forced businesspeople to accept the reality that business conducted over a computer, through video chat, is not only functional and normal but, in some cases, preferred. The pandemic proved that businesses and online relationships are a winning combination. The time is ripe to pair this new truth with a proven system like Predictive Social Media. The sky is the limit!

**Write the term or terms that best describe your category in Predictive Social Media.**

---

## MEET JIM

I'd much rather use this relationship-building space to listen and learn about you. Since that's not possible here, I'll tell you what I'd most want to know about a guy who claims that social media is predictive. Be sure to hop on your favorite platform afterward and find me so that I can meet you.

I've dedicated my entire career to social media. Before social media was a medium with a name and a guiding force in business, I was in the trenches. A client once told me that I'd probably forgotten more than most people would ever know about social media. That might be true. Twenty-five years, without detouring, is a long stretch on any one topic to make mistakes and learn and grow.

Lifelong learning is essential to me. Nothing stays. Everything changes. I recently graduated from Harvard Business School online and Babson College online. Knowledge is the first step to wisdom; sharing that knowledge is the first step of goodwill. Let's get acquainted so we can be that for each other.

I use my own system, every day, to build my business. Strange that I mention this, no? Many people claim to be social media experts but don't practice what they preach. First and foremost, I am my own customer. I use the system to grow businesses.

There are some gifted social media experts out there. Many of them built their success on specific products in a narrow silo of business. That's superb. I'm genuine when I say that I'm happy for them.

My route through social media in business has been more like the farm truck that travels from silo to silo—not necessarily by choice but as a result of where life has taken me. Opportunities that I once lamented became blessings for the experience they afforded me. I view social media through every lens of business—sole proprietor to global corporation.

Lastly, I want you to know that my system is crafted from a place of **heart**. It works across all industries in business, at all levels, but it also has far-reaching implications to make the world a better place. Charities and people who want to raise money to make life a little easier for others can use this system without any outlay of money because word of mouth is so much stronger than paid advertising. The system works to sell your home, to find readership for authors, and so much more. I can't wait for you to meet Jay. His quest for a kidney using the system brought him to a place he never imagined.

I met and fell in love with my wife, Marianne, using this system.

She might say otherwise.

**When I say this system has the power to change the world for good, I mean it.**

Let's change the world, together.

---

*Looking ahead:* Disruptive innovation is an often-misused catchphrase in business. In the next chapter, we examine the term's origins and explore how disruptive innovation plays a vital role in Predictive Social Media.

# CHAPTER TWO

## Disruptive Innovation

As a Harvard Business School online student, I was blessed to have been a student of Professor Clayton Christensen. In his 1997 book, *The Innovator's Dilemma*, which *The Economist* noted as one of the six most important business books ever written, Christensen outlined his groundbreaking theory on disruptive innovation.

To explain his concept, Christensen shared a story about two perceptions of God. One perception is that God exists outside the universe, like Zeus. God is bigger than the universe, so God can do things easily. The alternative perception is that God exists inside the universe and that God's power does not come from the position of being God, but rather the laws and forces and constraints that govern God, meaning that God can manipulate these factors to do remarkable things.

These two perceptions also apply to a company CEO.

Most people perceive a CEO as having power because of the position at the top of the company. Like Zeus, if the CEO wants something to happen, the CEO makes it happen. However, the CEO who exists inside the company, who understands the laws and forces and constraints of the business, harnesses all the power and does remarkable things.

Become the inside-the-universe CEO of your business and you will disrupt, not be disrupted.

The definition of disruptive innovation can be found on the internet, but it is wrong most of the time, and most people misuse the phrase. Maybe that's why most companies aren't disrupting anything while few are disrupting the most. Disruptive innovation is not innovation in support of whatever it is someone wishes to sell, nor does it mean to simply "shake up" an industry from what's been done before. These definitions are so broad as to be meaningless.

According to Christensen, the mastermind behind the concept, disruptive innovation is "The process in which a smaller company, usually with fewer resources, is able to challenge an established business (often called an *incumbent*) by entering at the bottom of the market and continuing to move up-market."[2] An innovative disruption strategy allows businesses to identify complex viewpoints, apply a strategic framework to assess new opportunities and potential threats, and acquire techniques for executive-level strategy formulation and team management.

Disruption is here.

Predictive Social Media allows businesses to identify complex viewpoints, delivers a strategic framework for new social media opportunity, and teaches techniques for strategy and team management. **Based on Christensen's definition, the Predictive Social Media system *is* disruptive innovation.**

Clayton broke disruptive innovation into theories, allowing us to view business differently. Some of these theories discuss sustaining innovation, low-end and new market disruption, good and bad money, and deliberate strategy. For this conversation, we'll apply his theory of *what job needs to be done*.

While companies with large marketing teams busy themselves with creating customer profiles for their products, disruptors who shift the business emphasis to relationships enjoy the most success. Thinking only about the product or service as the nucleus of acquiring and keeping customers leaves out the most fundamental question: *What job needs to be done?*

This question's shift in perspective is monumental for all stages and categories of business. Businesses no longer stuck on products and services open themselves to insights that get the job done, better and faster. Each new product or service is then based upon thoughts open to tomorrow, not mired in the limitations of today.

What I have developed delivers that tomorrow.

Predictive Social Media works. I created this system because I was its perfect customer. I asked, *What job needs to be done?* and found an effective way to implement. My solution is now yours.

## CATEGORIES AND DISRUPTION

Disruption is possible in all categories of business. Asking *what job needs to be done* turns trials into triumphs.

### INDEPENDENT CONTRACTORS

As a brand advocate in the direct sales industry, I've been down this road. It doesn't matter if you're selling jewelry on an e-commerce site, self-publishing novels, or repairing vintage clocks in your basement, or if you're an influencer posting videos on a favorite social media platform or a celebrity brand connecting with fans on social media—you're a one-person shop. The expectation to know how to do everything can feel like a burden.

Even if you enjoy the process of learning how to be a photographer and a writer and a marketer and a graphic designer and an accountant and dozens of other careers necessary for day-to-day operations, time spent away from your actual product or service slows growth. The fantasy of cloning yourself takes root. The pressure of success comes largely from within.

Today, I can do most things—not because I wanted to learn them but because I had to. That is the pressure of being an independent contractor.

### *What job needs to be done?*

You're alone. You don't have anyone to lean on to learn how to do social media the right way. The isolation and all you don't know is a struggle.

Most social media tools look at connection and communication with customers through a spyglass—detailed and helpful but narrow in focus. None of them take a step back to view the greater picture, to hold your hand every step of the journey, or to guarantee results the way Predictive Social Media does. When it comes to social media, you're no longer alone.

## SMALL BUSINESS OWNERS

I've owned two small businesses in my career: a software company and a PR agency. With small businesses, you gather specialty people to be part of your team and divide the workload. No longer are you expected to know how to do everything. With that freedom, burdens shift.

Resources are limited. Time is still at a premium because the buck stops with you. Investing in new technology or materials to grow competes with making payroll each month. Pressure expands to include the livelihood and well-being of your employees. One mistake could cause you to not make payroll. Sometimes, even in months you can afford payroll, you're left with a zero balance in your ledger. As such, your business decisions become cloaked in caution and fear.

### *What job needs to be done?*

You're looking for guarantees. You refuse to compromise the livelihood or happiness of your team. Investing in something to grow your product or service on social media that doesn't offer unbelievable returns isn't an option.

Predictive Social Media is where customer relationships meet math. Applying variables relevant to your unique business into a proven algebraic formula allows you to take calculated and guaranteed steps to move your business forward.

## LARGE CORPORATIONS

It's a heady feeling to have an army of workers behind your products and services. Aside from the astonishing number of meetings about meetings and the red tape involved with every decision, the corporate side of business makes good things happen in efficient and timely ways.

Stressors of moving parts and the ripple-effects of your decisions become the primary burden. Great ideas can lose momentum if they put the company at stake, and keeping everything highly organized becomes a necessity, not a luxury. Mistakes are magnified by big budgets and the loss of trust with your management team and employees that span the country or globe is a potential.

### *What job needs to be done?*

You have hundreds, if not thousands, of employees. You have the resources, money, and skills to take calculated risks to grow your company. Despite this, you still do not know which levers to pull, in order, to reduce your investment risk on social media.

More so than any other type of business, companies run on processes. Everything is calculated. Shouldn't you know which levers to pull to mitigate risk? Knowing, with precision, that input A yields output B aligns with the way you already run your business.

Social media initiatives should be no different.

The complexity of your business entity makes faulty decisions more likely and more damaging. Like a small business, you need guarantees. You're paid well so that massive missteps don't crumble the company.

Disruptive innovation is possible at all levels of business. Having a system that guarantees results is the key to effectively addressing the all-important question: *What job needs to be done?*

## PREDICTIVE CHECKLIST: DISRUPTIVE INNOVATION

❒ Disruptive innovation is the process by which a smaller company, usually with fewer resources, is able to challenge an established business (often called an "incumbent") by entering at the bottom of the market and continuing to move up-market.

❒ Instead of thinking about your product or service as the center of acquiring new customers, ask, *What job needs to be done?*

❒ Social media is low-cost and relationship-first.

———————

*Looking ahead:* The next two chapters fall under the umbrella of Contribution—the first of the 7Cs in Predictive Social Media. Value-based entrepreneurial thinking, relationship mindset, and personal growth were too extensive and impactful to fit into one chapter. These two chapters will push you beyond your comfort zone and are best encountered when you have time to absorb the system's underlying philosophy—perhaps over a weekend cup of coffee at your favorite spot—and not inside the rigid bustle of a workday.

No one approach to this book is correct. Bump around and experience the material your way. Thank you for joining me on your Predictive Social Media journey.

# CHAPTER THREE

## Contribution: Value-Based Entrepreneurial Thinking

I ONCE BUILT a social network to compete against MySpace and Facebook. Anyone of sound mind would not have attempted this.

In 2006, MySpace had 100 million users and surpassed Google as the most visited website. Facebook had 12 million users. No one believed site usage could grow much bigger. Today, two billion people use social media sites.

Had I been more educated, had I understood more about the space, I might not have attempted such a grand dream. My core value of *imagine* pushed me to do the impossible: an online world that replicated the real world. I wanted my site to be a place for entrepreneurs to connect with people online and mitigate the struggles they experienced offline, a place where everyone felt safe to mingle. I envisioned drag-and-drop customizable profiles, radio station feeds, a personal development portal to access trainers and coaches, and video features to rival the then-fledgling YouTube.

I found a man named Naveen on Myspace who was willing to outsource his tech experience to me. From India. But, *imagine*, right? Naveen's thumbs-up was enough to get me on a plane to Arizona to work with a company and build up the money to hire him. I was in my 20s, with little experience under my belt, but I generated a few hundred thousand dollars with this Arizona company in nine months.

As soon as I had the funds, I was on a plane to Ahmedabad, Gujarat, India.

I lived out of my comfort zone for three months, unable to speak Hindi or any of the other twenty-two languages in India, with no tech experience, no developer experience, no software experience, running only on the fuel of imagination that what Naveen and I were creating could be great.

What internal factor drove a kid on such an extreme voyage to tackle two Goliaths in the industry? Only someone driven by core values would complete such a journey.

I know what you're thinking: *Okay, so, there's no Hollywood ending here. I don't recall Jim Lupkin being a tech CEO at the same level as Mark Zuckerberg or Jack Dorsey. So much for core values.*

But wait. Are we not reframing success through its proper lens?

What is the price tag on personal growth?

One day, my business partner, Chetan, a Russian-American friend named Zachary, and I sat at a café, eating slices of cheese pizza and discussing software. Outside, five or six children, all bones, stared at the café patrons with vacant expressions. On the streets into work, I had already witnessed India's caste system. Cows grazed and laid waste at the same eight-foot-high trash piles where unwanted children scrounged for food. The horrific poverty had already led to sleepless nights. Weeks earlier, I had left the affluent real estate market of Arizona. The contrast made me physically ill. I couldn't take another moment without doing something.

On impulse, I purchased twelve pizzas and carried them out of the café. The children wouldn't take them. Instead, they cast guarded stares to three men gathered on the nearby street corner. Chetan charged out of the café and explained to me that the children were pawns, instructed to accept nothing but money by the men on the corner who owned them.

"I'm giving them pizza," I shouted at the men. "And they're going to eat it in front of us."

I was ready to throw down. They got one look at Zachary, who was as formidable as an ox, and they backed away. The three men stared us down the entire time those children ate, tears streaming down their dusty faces from finally having something in their bellies.

Business aside, those three months offered a more immersive experience in culture and sensitivity than most collect in a lifetime. I left materialism behind, found centeredness inside shrines and temples, and hung out with monkeys. As a naïve 20-something, I became a global citizen with an immersive background in tech—something that, to this day, still sets me apart from my closest competition. I talk social media from the marketing *and* tech side, while marketing guys only see the marketing view. As a result, I approach problems on social media and know instantly if the issue is a software bug on the platform's end or human error. To no small degree, this puts my clients at ease. Sometimes things happen beyond our control.

Those months, although far from perfect and definitely challenging, were an exquisite—albeit extreme—example of how living core values delivers you precisely where you are meant to be.

For the numbers-driven and curious among you, the social networking site that Naveen, Chetan, Zachary, and I created became the 17,000$^{th}$ most-visited site out of 85 million sites in the year we launched.

Should I have won, business-wise? No. I lacked the experience to win. But it showed me what was possible, on my resume and inside my soul.

## PERSONAL CORE VALUES

Entrepreneurial thinking is recognizing a problem, devising a solution, and assessing how many people will buy into that solution. If enough people want your solution, you start a business, make money, and grow.

For many entrepreneurs, this feels like success. But eventually, if this process fails to align with your core values, you won't find joy in success.

In this book, we focus on personal core values. Without a strong understanding of personal core values, company core values won't matter. Personal core values guide the thoughts, decisions, and actions that allow individuals to excel in business. Without attention to these core values, eventually, lives and businesses fall apart.

Until now, core values have rarely occupied the same conversation as entrepreneurship. **Traditionally, the business world isn't a touchy-feely space, rife with emotions and vulnerabilities. But as society leans into diversity, openness, and acceptance, businesses who don't embrace core values, who don't stand for something, will fall away.**

Businesses have a responsibility to articulate core values. Today's customers are savvy and seek truth in identity, and team members deserve to know if their employer's values match their personal values. It may seem obvious that an environmentally-conscious individual would never be satisfied working at an oil company or that a vegan would never find joy working for a cosmetic company that engages in animal testing, but I've consulted with enough stressed people to know that the lost among us don't always look to the disparity of core values as the root of their unhappiness.

Small businesses and companies who lean heavily on team members often find this concept most impactful. When company and personal values fall in-step, when day-to-day tasks and mini-projects take on a fresh energy viewed through a filter of values that positively impact the world, success is inevitable.

Independent contractors and brands may not have to worry about team members to optimize success, but even solopreneurs must evaluate how their company values align with their personal values. Where there is harmony, there is fulfillment far beyond a paycheck.

---

**Determine where you fit within the values of your business.**

▶ Make two columns. Try using a pen and paper. Your creative right brain needs love too.

▶ Write your five personal values in the left column. If you haven't yet zeroed in on your five core values or you need a little nudge to know if you went deep enough, be sure to check out the exercise at the end of the chapter.

▶ List your company's values in the right column. The landing page of the company's website is often a good starting point.

Study emails sent to customers, ad campaigns, logos, graphic designs, and materials passed down through the company hierarchy. Pay close attention to word patterns, phrases, and images that repeat and serve to reinforce these values.

▶ Beside the company's values, write down what those words or phrases mean to *you*.

▶ Remember I mentioned *glow* as one of my values? To me, *glow* means surrounding myself with positive people and things. I respect negativity but do not let it control me. To you, *glow* might mean something different.

▶ Reflect on the alignment of the two columns. How does working for your company, on your team, or solo allow you to live out your core values? Does your role allow you to work with authenticity?

If necessary, consider your most immediate project or your day-to-day duties. Do you find joy in your day, or do you dread it? Does the task take longer to complete than it should? Failing to identify joy means you'll always be on the lookout for something that aligns more closely with your core values—whether you recognize it or not.

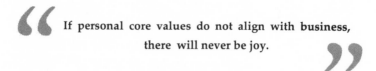

> If personal core values do not align with business, there will never be joy.

Top entrepreneurs fall in love with the process, not the end result. They find value in the everyday because it aligns with their core values. Predictive Social Media delivers joy because it allows you to live out your core values daily. Joy in the system is what delivers that 1 out of 5 ratio.

Many brand advocates I know chase carrots—usually trips to exotic destinations where the company foots the bill. They say they want to make five grand or ten grand a month, or they want to become millionaires. They spend years never finding success because they're not in love with the process.

**If you find entrepreneurship and work a tedious grind, your core values are not aligned with your business.**

Core values remain at the forefront of everything I do each day. At the bottom of each correspondence with my team, every virtual sticky note, I articulate those values. My team does the same. For each item on my to-do list, I ask myself, *Does this align with my core values?* If the answer is no, I reevaluate the focus of my business. If the answer is yes, doing the task makes me happy. Add up all that happiness, and I feel successful. Money no longer defines my success. Money is simply icing on the cake.

You've been led to believe that success is money. Numbers blind people and make them lose sight of the big picture. Now is the time for grassroots, all-in, honest-to-goodness shift away from believing that your bank account determines your worth.

Contrary to what you might think, millionaires and billionaires—at least the ones I've encountered in my career—do not sit around all day talking about money. Their true currency is engaging people, finding joy in actively participating in something meaningful, and being an integral part of the human experience.

Some might say that freedom from worry about money gives wealthy people the luxury to find joy elsewhere. To that, I answer that the joy they found in their process, made possible by living their core values, led to their wealth.

**Acquiring wealth is no guarantee of joy; acquiring joy guarantees joy. When your time on this earth runs out, what's more likely to be on your mind: what's in your wallet or the memories and evidence of core values you cherished in this lifetime?**

> Chasing money leads nowhere; chasing core values helps you make more money than ever before and brings joy to your life.

Embrace that road of revenue and customer acquisition and every other granular aspect of growing a business, but understand that for true happiness, core values must be part of your story.

For predictive success in social media, core values must be your driving force.

## SEASONS OF VALUES

Values change based on our season in life. Life experiences and age are two biggies that reshape our values.

Throughout my life, *inspire* and *imagine* were persistent core values. *Enlighten* was there, as well. *Truth*? That core value snuck up on me.

The old me often justified things and avoided confrontation. I valued truth, but for reasons that still aren't clear, I rarely stood my ground until my mom died. Losing her sharpened my vision for life. Where once, I awoke and obsessed over impeccable clothes to make a good business impression, I began to dress and move on with my day. I viewed authenticity, not the ideals society dictated for me, as my ultimate currency. The voice I had suppressed emerged. Her death taught me that time is too limited in this life to spend one moment living anything but my truth.

Ten years ago, I didn't understand core values, much less how to properly activate them in my life. In retrospect, I was on the right path; yet, I fueled myself with the *emotion* of my core values—something very different. During setbacks, I felt overwhelmed and frustrated, preferring to wallow in my sadness, and then failed to understand how emotions defeated my dreams.

Now, when I find myself in a negative place, no matter the emotion, I remember my core values and remind myself why I'm in the situation. I ask, *Do I want to stay or get out?* That question, that authority to choose the *real* me, never fails to bring peace to my restlessness.

I meet handcuffed people all the time. They're angry and unfulfilled. They focus on things that don't reflect their core values. "I want to quit," they tell me. So, we break down their core values. When they realize their core values have nothing to do with the things that occupy their energy and time, it's heart and clarity and life, all rolled into one spectacular ray of hope. Helping people regain a sense of control and get back in touch with their genuine self is one of the most joyous parts of my system.

Values don't roll in and out with the tides, but they do shift. The key is to elevate your awareness and be ready to pivot.

## THE PIVOT

Changing jobs and careers isn't always practical, but it is possible to pivot inside your situation until you're ready to make a more permanent change.

First, recognize the need for change. **If you're in a bad life situation, it's because you're not living your core values.** Live authentically, every single day, based on your core values, and you'll never be in a lousy position in life.

Next, identify at least *one* core value to start. Try the exercise at the end of this section. Maybe start with the phrase, "I am happy when I . . ." and don't stop until you've landed on an answer that sends a warm vibration up your spine. Core values are an internal frequency. You'll know when you're close. Write down that *one* core value in a location you see several times a day—on your refrigerator, on your phone's lock screen, scrawled across a sticky note affixed to your car's dashboard, or written on your bathroom mirror with a dry-erase marker.

Before you make decisions in your day, ask yourself, *How does this align or conflict with my one core value?* If it conflicts, don't do it. Or if you must do it, you've elevated your awareness and understand why you're triggered. Big frustrations happen when people don't understand the reason behind negative emotions.

Gradually expand that one core value to five. Keep the list together in places you'll see often. Reflect on how these five core values fit with each other and how closely they align with the life you're living.

Inside the parameters of what is expected of you, it is possible to shift your mindset to embrace your five core values. Managing or redefining expectations can be as simple as communicating your new outlook to your coworkers or leaders.

Find ways outside of business to meet your core values so you feel closer to whole until you're ready to make a permanent change. Understand, however, true joy comes from embracing core values in all areas of life.

*Inspire. Imagine. Truth. Glow. Enlighten.*

Above are my core values. Undoubtedly, over time, these five will evolve to reflect future challenges and experiences. Find me on social media and share your five values. I'd love to hear them. If you still need an idea boost after the exercise below, be sure to turn to Appendix A, where you'll find a list of value words to inspire you.

There I go again, living my core values.

---

Discovering your core values is like being an automobile passenger on a familiar route. While driving necessitates a tunnel-like attention on the road to scan for lane markers and hazards, being a passenger allows us to see the bigger picture out the windshield: the angle of falling maple leaves on the wind, how clouds sometimes look like spilled cotton balls after a storm, the precise shade of wildflowers along a neighbor's fence.

In life, we're often devoted to keeping our eyes on the road. Become a passenger for a moment. I'll drive.

Open your bank and charge accounts. Study the last two months of purchases. The things you bought align with your core values. Make notes and dive deeper. Ask yourself *why* you made those purchases. A recurring Thursday night dinner isn't just a tasty lasagna at your favorite little Italian place when you realize it was a step toward healing a fractured relationship or an opportunity to demonstrate appreciation and love to your spouse who cooks dinner all the other nights of the week.

Follow the same process with your cell phone. Study the photos and videos in your camera roll. Your core values are there, in the images you keep.

## CORE VALUES IN LEADERSHIP

How many of you have buzzword fatigue?

I'm raising my hand with you.

Every few years, a thought-leader flexes a philosophy to fill another bestseller and the buzz starts. Everyone flocks to conferences with heavily produced light shows. What was once a *what-if* question in the thought-leader's mind trickles down to workers, far removed from the idea's origin. Having run its course, the book crowds the bargain bin at the grocery store and the cycle starts anew.

Leadership is far less smoke-and-mirrors. **For me, leadership is showing others what's possible by doing it yourself.** Since one of my core values is *inspire*, my leadership style is organic to me.

My definition of leadership may not be your definition, and that's okay. Core values act as colored lenses, tinting and shading how we view reality. In fact, I'm willing to bet you can craft your perfect definition of leadership based on your core value list.

Leadership, then, is the union of core values to action.

Everyone running a business, from start-up to a multi-billion-dollar organization, navigates through evolving plans, market volatility, current events that shift perception, board members who have different ideas, and a hundred other challenges to their initial vision. How do leaders assign core values to such a large entity? Is it possible?

The answer is an emphatic yes.

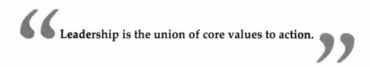

**Leadership is the union of core values to action.**

Most successful people don't have conversations about core values; they're successful because they're subconsciously living their core values.

Core values isn't a new concept. There have always been words for what we're talking about here: passion, gumption, grit, hunger. What feels fresh is the impact of core values on business.

## REFLECTION

Jim's definition of leadership: *the union of core values to action.*

My definition of leadership:

**How does your definition of leadership reflect your core values?**

---

**How can you uniquely bring value to others?**

---

## PREDICTIVE CHECKLIST: VALUE-BASED ENTREPRENEURIAL THINKING

❐ Business *shouldn't* be about selling a product or service.

❐ Predictive Social Media takes trust between people and applies a systematic and mathematical component to harness the true power of relationships.

❐ Successful people live their core values.

❐ Businesses have a responsibility to articulate core values to customers and team members.

❐ Values change based on our season in life.

❐ Before you make decisions in your day, ask yourself, *How does this align or conflict with my core values?*

*Looking ahead:* To be successful with Predictive Social Media, you must take a few skeletons out of the closet and dance with them. You'll see what I mean in chapter four, the second part of Contribution: Personal Growth and Relationships. The next portion of Contribution is all about conquering the barriers within to finally achieve remarkable things—in business and in life. Acknowledging shortcomings can be scary. Rejection is painful. But with a closer look through the frame of my system, limitations start to look like opportunities.

# CHAPTER FOUR

## Contribution: Personal Growth and Relationships

ONE OF MY business clients came to me in a fired-up state. She was convinced her primary competition was poaching her customers. The two women began their relationship harmoniously, partnering up to do live events on social media, but as success in one business increased, my client entrepreneur grew concerned that she had a target on her back.

After I conducted a thorough social media autopsy, I determined that the evidence my client handed over to me did not correlate with the narrative in her head. "Forget about her," I said. "She's insignificant. Let's focus on building your success."

I thought that was the end of it.

My client could not let it go. She spent long periods of time looking through the other woman's online pages to gather more evidence—largely circumstantial—and prove what she suspected.

Finally, I called out my client. Had she spent time dedicated to growing her business instead of trying to prove something was amiss with her competition, her benchmark achievements in Predictive Social Media might have come sooner. She realized that obsessing over something she had failed to prove did not align with her core values and left that distraction behind for good. Her personal growth allowed her to move on to bigger and better things.

# PERSONAL GROWTH

Once you understand what makes you tick, your core values, you'll build fast relationships based on things that bring you joy. While this new connectedness brings excitement and a level of self-awareness you may not have experienced before, it can also magnify personality traits we'd rather not share with the world.

To win with Predictive Social Media, confront undesirable traits in your personality. Ask yourself hard questions. In business and in life, what prevents you from moving forward? What behaviors distance you from others? Do your people or communication skills need work? What needs, beliefs, and fears keep you from your essence?

Settle for nothing less than truth.

Recall the Pareto Principle portion of the formula. Twenty percent of people are responsible for 80% of the action. Those 20% find ways to eliminate the human error in the formula. Imagine your success when you do the same.

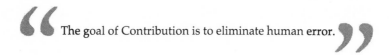 The goal of Contribution is to eliminate human error.

# FEARS

Psychologist Karl Albrecht believes that fear is nothing more than information.

"Medical experts tell us that the anxious feeling we get when we're afraid is a standard biological reaction. It's pretty much the same set of body signals, whether we're afraid of getting bitten by a dog, getting turned down for a date, or getting our taxes audited," Albrecht explains. "Fear, like all other emotions, is basically information. It offers us knowledge and understanding—if we choose to accept it."[3]

Albrecht outlines five basic human fears, a "feararchy" play off of Maslow's famous needs hierarchy, from which all other fears derive. At the most basic level, humans experience fear of extinction and mutilation—death or harm. It is in the upper three stages, however, where human connection factors into fear.

Loss of autonomy ushers in a fear of being trapped or immobile. Claustrophobia—the fear of tight spaces—is a manifestation of this fear on a physical level. On an emotional level, feeling smothered can hold people back from forming and maintaining relationships.

Separation is also a basic human fear. Everything that comes along with the notion of loss, including abandonment and rejection, can make people feel disrespected and devalued. This fear can be especially potent inside social media, where group dynamics play a role in our connectedness.

Albrecht's final basic fear is known as *ego-death*. He defines *ego-death* as, "The fear of humiliation, shame, or any other mechanism of profound self-disapproval that threatens the loss of integrity of the self; the fear of the shattering or disintegration of one's constructed sense of lovability, capability, and worthiness."[3]

While base fears have survival value, many fears are learned behavior—nothing more than micro-flitters of reaction that relate back to a traumatic memory. As such, they can be revisited, placed into proper perspective, and unlearned.

In a social media system based on relationships, any one of these three stages of Albrecht's feararchy have the capacity to derail the most well-intentioned entrepreneur.

Understanding fears diminishes their power.

## FEAR OF REJECTION

Mr. Secara was one of *those* teachers. The kind you carry with you through adulthood, packed in the front of your memories because they taught you far more than four walls and a textbook could hold. He taught senior year economics, encouraged me to compete in regional and state competitions, and gave me additional books and tutorials when I doubted myself.

For an entire semester, I tried to pitch him my long-distance phone service. Yes, I'm old enough for that to have been a thing people purchased. Each time I mustered the courage to darken his classroom door after school, I chickened out. My heart raced and my pores leaked sweat. My legs refused to carry me to his desk with my presentation materials in hand. Though Mr. Secara represented everything I didn't know about business, my inability to cross that threshold had nothing to do with him. He was kind and nurturing; I was a mess of rejection panic.

One day toward the end of the final semester, I stood in the empty hallway for thirty minutes, listening to the scratching and sorting sounds of him grading papers. The school felt like a blast furnace. I ran through a million scenarios in my head, most of them ending with Mr. Secara laughing or a fire alarm clearing the building. The bundle of marketing materials in my arms—brochures, presentation books, VHS tape—felt like an anchor that kept me from moving forward. Finally, I took one step in the room.

Mr. Secara glanced up. His expression illuminated like a bulb, and he smiled. "Hey, Jim."

At eighteen, my small-talk skills left a little to be desired. I launched in like napalm, loud and messy. "Would you check this stuff out and tell me what you think?" I said then dumped my arm load on his desk.

To Mr. Secara's credit, he didn't flinch. He simply said, "Sure."

I'd like to say that we had a great business chat, that I answered his questions, that he imparted some great economic wisdom that I still carry to this day, that I signed him up for long distance right then, but that wouldn't be a real story about the fear of rejection. In the spirit of keeping it real, I'll tell you that after he uttered that one word—sure—I bolted out of his classroom like someone had pulled the fire alarm. Not my finest moment.

Fear of rejection is real, and I had an acute case of it in high school. The only reason I walked into that classroom, eventually, was because I believed in my services. I used them myself and saw the savings every month.

If you use the system correctly, rejection isn't personal. When someone says no to your product or service, they're doing just that— saying no to products and services, not you.

When you feel rejected in business, one of three things happened:

1. The person saying no hasn't yet had the life experience to take advantage of your business.
2. You haven't inspired them to be part of your business. In

short, you must show the person you are passionate about your product, service, and business. If you demonstrate that belief through your actions, you will inspire others.

3. The person rejecting simply doesn't connect with you. Think about two women, equally passionate about sports. One lives and breathes scuba diving. The other knows everything there is to know about rock climbing. In no way does the experience associated with these sports overlap. The commonalities aren't there, so their time is best spent connecting with those whom they can build a relationship.

Underlying reasons for someone saying no can be as varied as the reasons someone says yes. If you internalize those reasons, fear clouds you from the truth.

Remember that one cool house in your neighborhood as a kid? Mine was the Halsey residence, which had a huge yard for tackle football. Everyone hung out there. Once, during those cringe-worthy years of junior high, the Halsey boy in my grade had a sleepover. Despite hanging out there nearly every day after school, I wasn't invited. I felt totally rejected. In an epic knee-jerk reaction known only to me, I stopped going over there.

Two weeks later, while grocery shopping with my mom, I ran into Mrs. Halsey. She had a brilliant British accent that could simultaneously make you feel like a nitwit and the Prince of England. She asked where I had been and said, "Hope ya not stayin' away due to the sleepovah. Just didn't have the room on mah floor. Bodies everywhere. Smelly ones, at that." She patted me on the shoulder. "Come 'round soon."

Mrs. Halsey hadn't rejected me. She merely had a logistics problem. A "smelly one, at that." Who knows what kind of epic milestones of pre-adolescence I missed out on during those two weeks when rejection clouded the truth?

If you have a fear of rejection, deal with it immediately. It can, and will, cripple your business. Be brave and fearless. Don't stand outside the door or sit on the sidelines because you're afraid someone may say no. It only takes one opportunity to change your life. Don't lose a special chance because you were afraid to be rejected.

Rejection is especially brutal when it's face to face (or voice to voice on a phone call). Social media lessens the risk of awkward encounters and uncomfortable phone conversations. Platform interactions allow you to reach out to people in a safer way in a timeframe that benefits both parties. Some would argue that it's easier on social media to be ghosted—meaning no response. That may be true, but not hearing back from someone via direct messages on the social platform of your choice stings far less than a personal encounter where you receive an outright, "No. I'm not interested." And if your friend responds via social media with, "Not interested, but thanks for checking in," and you're following the social media system, you'll recognize this for what it is: one of the three components isn't yet in place but there is still a warm connection to continue to nurture into friendship.

## FEAR OF PUBLIC SPEAKING

According to Psychology Today, nearly one-quarter of all people have some fear of public speaking.[4] Much of this anxiety is triggered by overstimulation in the nervous system. Learning techniques to place yourself in a calm state can counteract the physiological response brought on by speaking to an audience, but what if this fear runs deeper?

Negative associations with past public speaking events—failed oral reports, bad play performances, awkward acceptance speeches, and any other time in our childhood when we encountered a less-than-favorable audience—carry far into adulthood and cause us to avoid situations where we might have to speak publicly. Unfortunately, this avoidance gets in the way of success for people who can make the world a better place by sharing their intelligence and gifts.

The running dialog you allow inside your thoughts in these public speaking moments also has a significant impact. If you perceive that your audience is better—more intelligent, more liked, more beautiful—your speaking ability suffers. Cognitive reframing and positive affirmation are two ways to counteract these damaging thought patterns.

Predictive Social Media takes the emphasis away from performance and puts it squarely back into communication.

## FEAR OF JUDGMENT

Another common fear is worry about what others think of you. In business, this can manifest as not speaking up at meetings when you have something important to say and failing to ask for a raise that's long overdue.

Humans are inherently judgmental. What others think will always be beyond your control, so why allow anyone's opinion to dictate your day? Being liked 100% of the time is an impossibility. With 7.6 billion people on the planet, odds are favorable that you'll find someone whose personality doesn't mesh with yours. Instead of carefully orchestrating who you allow into your life based on how likely they are to judge you, embrace the idea that their responses are impossible to anticipate and completely irrelevant.

Predictive Social Media is designed such that the people who gravitate toward you become genuine friends. If people judge you when they look at your profile, they simply won't respond to your request, thus removing the sting of open judgment, such as someone laughing at you. You won't feel the negativity. Instead, you'll be surrounded by people who enter into relationships with you because they want to be with you.

## WORDS

Are you sharing your business with the fewest words? People often take the long route when communicating about something that brings them joy, which can turn people off. An economy of words—crisp, actionable, confident—conveys the power of your convictions while also respecting others' time.

Are your words phrased in a positive light? Negative words can trigger people, especially in the world of social media, where people have been conditioned to slip into a mental suit of armor every time they log in. **Your words have the power to become someone's emotional gravity for the day. Make sure that gravity is positive.**

Ashley and I have many mutual friends and both love helping others, but a negative social trait of hers keeps us from forming a deeper connection. She loves to drop names instead of focusing on solving problems. She often says things like, "You know I know Richard from ABC, right? He's going to help. By the way, I also know Sam from XYZ. Check out my phone's contact list. See for yourself. I have his number!" Ashley thinks nothing of ambushing television celebrities for her social media podcast and putting them on the spot. Her business world is often carefully outlined in black and white.

Despite Ashley's tendency to brag about her contacts, I maintain a connection with her. We live in the same city, have many mutual friends, and have a common interest. We've visited some of the same vacation destinations and shared photographs. Every time I meet with her, I say, "Focus, my friend. No name dropping. Let's solve this problem." Ashley laughs. She no longer drops names around me. Together, we focus on solving problems.

Everyone has skeletons. Successful people find ways to move past them. What a shame it would be to have an enlightened view of your values and a talent for friendships, but a fear of failure or public speaking holds you back from greatness.

Predictive Social Media works—even with human error factored in. Addressing areas of needed growth and becoming a better person brings you into the fullness of who you are meant to be.

One of the first companies I went to work for as a brand advocate emphasized personal development. We'd pack conference rooms in Cherry Hill, New Jersey, and spend the entire day squirming in our skin from self-reflection. Back then, for a company to advocate for the mental health and personal struggles of its brand advocates was unprecedented and led to an explosive time in my growth and philosophy. Fear of rejection, believing in yourself, the right to feel capable of anything—you name it, we covered it.

In this system, you will sink or soar based on your interpersonal skills. People need to like you. **Getting an honest read on your shortcomings can be a challenge.** The following exercise may offer insight.

**The 10/5/5 List**

**Step 1**: Write ten words to describe yourself. Although business may be an important part of your life, lean into who you are when you're not conducting business.

**Step 2**: Select two people who know you well. A spouse. A child. A good friend. Ask them to list five words to describe you.

**Step 3**: Select two people who don't know you as well. These are acquaintances with whom you come into contact occasionally but whose opinions you value. Ask these two people to list five words to describe you.

**Step 4**: Gather the word lists in front of you. Are there parallels? Inconsistencies? Highlight positive words in one color and negative words in a different color. Do the majority of positive words come from within or from the outside? The more the words in this exercise align, the closer you are to living and projecting your authentic self. If that authentic self needs work, do the work.

This exercise never fails to amaze me. People often see things in me I cannot see in myself. Personal growth doesn't only happen in a conference space in Cherry Hill, New Jersey; it happens every day, in every encounter, in the running narrative inside my head each morning, and in every decision I make while interacting.

## RELATIONSHIPS

When artists set out to create a work of art, they often sketch geometric lines on paper or canvas. Although the observer rarely sees these shapes in the end product, the lines provide a framework upon which a masterpiece is crafted. So long as the artist adheres to these invisible lines, the freedom of creativity around them is immense.

Predictable social media provides the lines. The system is timing, sequence, and process—a framework upon which your social media masterpiece is crafted. But like an artist to canvas, freedom of creativity is yours. The relationship portion of the system is where your imagination soars.

Relationships are an art. Like artists, we must enter into social media each day, pressing brush to canvas to create, together. Art doesn't just happen; quality relationships do not just happen. **Each new day marks a profound choice about how we interact with the world.**

Socially, we are poised to emerge from an age of negativity.

High expectations and disappointing outcomes in everything from politics to societal issues have the power to dictate our moods and behaviors. Perhaps most damaging, negativity has seeped into our emotional support systems, our families, and our intimate relationships, leading to an unprecedented mental health crisis.

But negativity is on its way out. How do I know this?

If you look in the right places, you'll discover it's already gone.

Videos that touch heartstrings go viral. Social media challenges raise money for charity. Positivity in the human condition moves people to act, to think, to purchase. Companies that embrace the connectedness we all share, that view the interaction between product or service and customer as something that happens not *for*, but *with*, alongside, and companies that view solidarity as one of the most coveted states of being are the businesses that experience supernova expansion.

Relationships court optimism.

The traditional game of business is an artificial way of being. People are hardened to the rules and weary of how some players manipulate outcomes. What if business was no longer a game but viewed through the long-overdue lens of genuine connection? What if businesses based their decisions on core values? What if brand advocates and influencers allowed the artificial lines between work and life to blur so that they simply existed inside a space of authenticity?

**What if we redefined success to simply being better humans?**

This concept wasn't always so second-nature to me. In my young entrepreneurial days, I viewed nearly everyone as a transaction. Before they were men or women carrying grief or exploring their identity or fighting to be seen and heard, before it registered with me that they had a heartbeat and dreams and challenges I couldn't begin to imagine, I viewed them as a potential customer or brand advocate. I had bought into the traditional game of business at the expense of my humanity. I was nineteen. I wanted to be like the people around me. I was told their lives were the lives to emulate.

As life has a way of doing, it recently brought me back into contact with this painful lesson from my past. Near the end of my mother's life, while she spent a few months in rehabilitation, I ran into an old friend in our town's nursing home. Two decades after my narrow-minded ambition had fractured our relationship, he barely looked me in the eye. We exchanged canned pleasantries. I was pretty sure he'd have rather sat in his cold car in the snowstorm stirring beyond the windows than talk to me. How different that exchange might have been had I focused on putting our relationship first all those years ago. Standing in the stale air, trying not to cry through those moments of fear and grief at watching my mother slip away, I didn't need a customer or a brand advocate. I needed a friend.

———

**Business can't just be about selling a product or service.**

**Business shouldn't be about selling a product or service.**

———

Before you dismiss this notion, before you dismiss me as a dreamer and an idealist whose feet never touch the ground, before you dismiss my years of experience in social media that unequivocally proves that relationships build the best businesses, take a moment to consider the relationship-first revolution we already see in our world.

- Executives who have a social media presence enjoy a greater following than the companies they represent.
- Employees of major corporations whose social media presence align with company values are being asked to continue their day-in-the-life social media posts as brand advocates (at great risk to the company, when one public misstep could turn into a public relations nightmare).
- A star investor and real estate mogul of the most-watched entrepreneurial television show in the US invites potential hires to meet her existing sales team first and pitches her product second.

A venture capital firm recently contacted me to ask if I had interest in spearheading the launch of a new company that has the ability to show the virility of social media posts—basically, how to scale word of mouth online. My answer was short and sweet. I've already figured it out and have the system.

Venture capital firms are significant players in the world of business. Why would institutions like this be willing to put down massive amounts of money in the pursuit of scaling relationships online? Because they know it will change the world of business forever.

People want to be connected to people.

Challenging the status quo in business is understanding that you might have a great product or service with quality ingredients or features at a great price, but those markers are still black and white parameters. Social media has taught us that a list of features no longer sells products. Consumers in today's world may look at factors such as ingredients and price; but, almost always, they look at reviews. **People make decisions based on trust.** Even if they have no relationship with the reviewer, social proof is a driving consumer force.

The business world is only beginning to talk about relationships. **Until now, no metrics existed to determine if investing in relationships played a direct role in desired outcomes.** And if a relationship-based method worked, it was nearly impossible to scale. As a result, company marketing teams gravitate toward metrics they're able to control and analyze and leave the touchy-feely bit of human interaction to therapists and life coaches.

Social media allows the idea of relationships in business. Predictive Social Media takes age-old wisdom—the essence of human trust and influence—and applies a systematic and mathematical component to harness and scale the true power of relationships.

Think about your business relationships. Why do you have a great relationship with your supplier? Why do you invest time to develop good relationships with your colleagues and other influencers in your industry? Why do you cultivate good relationships with your team and their families? Why bother with these relationships?

Because if you don't, you won't make it.

Intuitively, you already know this. You're already nurturing relationships. But when you put on your business hat each morning, that mindset vaporizes in favor of how traditional business has always been conducted, in favor of the black and white, because it's familiar and safe and doesn't feel so vulnerable.

Think about Elon Musk and Jeff Bezos. Elon Musk was an original founder of PayPal. He also founded Tesla and SpaceX. Tesla's success forced every major car manufacturer in the world to develop an electric car. Prior to SpaceX, the only entities capable of launching rockets into space were world governments. Jeff Bezos is the founder of Amazon, one of the first trillion-dollar companies in the history of business. Who doesn't shop on Amazon?

Some of you may not be fond of these men for personal reasons. That's okay. Understand, however, that their companies are built on relationships. They don't lean heavily on advertising to sell their products. They exist inside a network they've forged and allow word of mouth to sell for them.

In your product or service niche, become the Elon Musk or Jeff Bezos. Focus on impeccable relationships. Aim to illuminate your corner of the business world. Lift others—employees, customers, suppliers, executives—and you'll enter into the fullness of success—however you define that term.

This light is only the beginning of the system's power.

Soon, anyone who touches your business will join your hope-filled community, a virtual space that runs twenty-four hours a day, seven days a week on social media, when you're not present. Relationships grow exponentially stronger and faster inside the light of your product or service than you ever imagined.

People long to be part of something inspiring and genuine.

Make your business that safe space to usher in the coming age of optimism.

## SOCIAL MEDIA RELATIONSHIP TIPS

By now, you're gaining an understanding of the crucial nature of relationships in Predictive Social Media. For those who want to start strengthening relationships today, here are some quick wins.

- Always think, *How do I provide value in this person's life, with everything I say and everything I do?* When someone randomly pops into your thoughts or something reminds you of a person, don't let it go. Shoot that person a message on social media. Something as simple as, *You've been on my mind today. Just wanted to say hello.* Ten seconds. That's all it takes to advance a relationship. From a pure place inside you, it's all about making others feel better and happier because you're in their lives.
- As you progress in the system, you'll be learning how to have effective one-on-one conversations with others. Become an expert at asking meaningful questions. Allow the other person to talk. In a twenty-minute conversation, yield fifteen minutes to the other person. This may seem excessive, but people love the sound of their voice and the extra time you dedicate to others gives you opportunities to get to know them as people. Listen and remember ways that your product or service might benefit them based on what they say. Talking about yourself and taking over the conversation causes people to put up walls. You're not selling to people; you're building relationships.
- Use the other person's first name while conversing. Names conveys warm, open feelings of respect and recognition. For those among us who tend to instantly forget names after an

introduction, name reinforcement in your brain also makes you a better friend.

- Smile. Sounds *so* simple, yet many of us forget to do it while on video or live feeds. Children smile, on average, four hundred times per day, while adults smile twenty times per day. Get in touch with your inner child. Place a reminder to smile on a sticky note beside your camera or phone.

## PREDICTIVE CHECKLIST: PERSONAL GROWTH AND RELATIONSHIPS

❒ To be successful with Predictive Social Media, you must take a hard look at areas of your personality that need improvement.

❒ Fear, like all other emotions, is information that offers us knowledge and understanding.

❒ Understanding fears diminishes their power.

❒ Taking the emphasis away from performance and emphasizing communication can help overcome public speaking anxiety.

❒ In this system, you will sink or soar based on your people skills. People need to like you.

❒ The words you share with others should be positive and concise for maximum impact.

❒ The goal of Contribution is to eliminate human error.

*Looking ahead:* Any fuel you put in your car's gas tank will probably get you where you want to go, but imagine how much smoother and more efficient the ride when you choose quality fuel to maximize an engine's performance. Proficiency in your chosen platform is that fuel, and it's essential for Predictive Social Media to work at an optimum level. The next of the 7Cs—Capabilities—offers criteria for choosing the best site for your unique business and helps you close the knowledge gaps that may be holding you back.

## HOW MANY PLATFORMS?

Time is finite. With only so many hours in the day, the thought of hopping on platform after platform is daunting—not to mention that the system is designed to make you more efficient with your time so you can put your phones down, step away from your laptops, and live out your core values in the real world.

I'm often asked how many platforms a business should implement into their social media plan. My answer almost always relates to the category of business.

## LARGER BRANDS AND COMPANIES

The goal of this category is to get the word out to social media in a big way. Large brands and companies have more money, resources, and team members to ensure a consistent presence on chosen platforms. Selecting multiple platforms with the most users makes sense. Investigate recent data regarding the demographic of worldwide users on each platform. Choose platforms where your customers live.

## INDEPENDENT CONTRACTORS, INFLUENCERS, BRAND ADVOCATES, AND SMALL BUSINESSES

Your time is extremely limited. Focus on *one* platform and implement it to expert levels. Choose the site that has the most users to form the greatest relationships in the shortest time. As with larger brands and companies, your product or services may play a substantial role in dictating which platform you choose. Use more than one platform if— and only if—you are already using that separate platform for personal reasons. Chances are, if you find joy in spending time with an alternate site, applying the Cs will be effortless.

Success in one platform does not guarantee success in the next. The likelihood that you'll be able to replicate your first platform's success when you jump to another site is slim. Begin to look at your limited time as your most valuable resource. Focusing that resource behind what already works makes good business sense.

## NAVIGATING HURRICANES

By its nature, social media innovates and evolves. Every now and then, major platforms introduce sweeping changes. Similar to a hurricane forming in the vast ocean of social media, these changes may be forecast in the short term but often leave users little time to react. The impact can devastate businesses who are unprepared to weather the storm.

Predictive Social Media is your fortified boat.

If a platform overhaul leaves you feeling lost, if you feel frustrated that you must start your business again on the platform, it's a strong indication that you didn't understand that platform's essence on a deep enough level to adapt to changes. All platforms have a philosophy and a pulse. To be successful on any platform, you must understand the site's soul.

Approach the platform with an eye to discovery. Spend time clicking around new areas. Practice features by being playful with close friends and family so you can use those same features with confidence in a business setting. Interact with the site on different devices. Take note of how to perform features that align perfectly with the 7Cs so you can utilize them until they become intuitive. Learn what you do not know.

I am always surprised at people who are willing to pay a third party to learn the ins and outs of a platform. All social media sites have free tutorials tucked inside their interface. Who better to tutor users than those who understand the site's philosophy and soul?

---

Jessica runs a horse-and-tack business in upstate New York. She enjoyed moderate success inside a popular social media site for several years. While she questioned some fundamentals about the platform, she never took the time to overcome those deficits in her knowledge. She was far too busy running her small business.

Then the platform introduced sweeping changes.

The evolution of the site baffled her. Jessica could no longer keep up with the changes. Her business suffered. She came to me with a laundry list of site-related issues that had compromised her income.

Together, we implemented the Predictive Social Media system.

Jessica's life changed when she began living her core values. Her business now represents creativity, community, authenticity, and love. **Every social media interaction is more than a sale; each customer represents an opportunity to pay forward the transformative moments and unyielding support in her life.** Her live events are legendary. Don't get me started on her female customers swapping cowboy stories and photos.

In four months, Jessica's business went from $28,000 in one-month sales to over $88,000 per month. In that short period of time, her laundry list of site issues disappeared. It wasn't always a matter of us deliberately tackling her platform problems like a checklist; rather, the system taught Jessica how to use the platform the right way and her site issues subsided. She developed a respect and understanding about the platform she didn't have before the changes. Now, when the platform evolves again, Jessica will be ready.

## SPECIAL PLATFORMS

Some social media sites fall outside the typical offerings and deserve special mention. Foremost in my mind are platforms that lean heavily on video content. At first glance, it may seem like these platforms don't fit into Predictive Social Media because interaction with friends does not follow the pattern of more traditional social media sites. So long as the areas of Conversation, Community, Connection, and Communication are present, the system will work.

---

*Conversation* – the ability to have authentic and robust interactions about your personal and business life with your social media friends.

*Community* – the place on social media where people can hear from others who love your product or service.

*Connection* – accessing an endless supply of potential customers and people who will refer your business to others while building real relationships.

*Communication* – staying in touch the right way to build enduring relationships for your business to thrive.

---

Consider how each of the above 4Cs may require adaptation for these special platforms:

- Although videos feature you, your life, and your business—very you-centered—does the platform provide ways to give your followers a voice so they can have a personalized *conversation* with you and with each other?
- Is there a way, on or off-platform, to develop those followers into a dedicated *community*?
- Is there an endless supply of potential customers with whom you can forge a *connection*?
- Does the platform offer *communication* features that allow you to stay in touch the right way so you can continue to build warm relationships?

If the answer to these questions is yes, a special platform might be the perfect way for your product or service to implement Predictive Social Media.

## SOCIAL MEDIA PLATFORM CONSIDERATION

Does the platform have the capabilities that allow you to properly implement the system?

_____

Is it possible to create and nurture a community on this platform?

_____

What features allow you to have one-on-one conversations with friends?

_____

Does the interface allow you to connect with large numbers of people —the kind that you would want as friends in real life?

_____

What is the longevity factor? Does your content disappear soon after it's posted or does it allow for relationships with friends in other time zones around the world to work for you, even when you're not on social media?

_____

How do the platform's standout features fit into the system and optimize your business?

_____

Does the platform's culture match the culture of your product or service?

_____

Can you navigate this platform with ease? Do you have time to learn the site's fundamentals so that you can implement to its full potential?

_____

As a general rule, the largest and most popular platforms will be the most conducive to the system. These platforms grew in popularity for a reason. They offer the widest array of options and the greatest opportunity for impact.

Does that mean you should completely disregard a platform if you enjoy using it but find it lacking in one of the critical C elements? Not necessarily. Maybe there's an off-platform way to implement the missing Cs through other interfaces and technology. This may add an extra step to your business, but it's important for you to recognize now that this system is not rigid. Allow it to flex and work for you when you bring it into the fold of your business. Understanding the Cs on a deep level means you can adapt the system's principles and methods to any platform.

## PREDICTIVE CHECKLIST: CAPABILITIES

❐ Knowing the fundamentals of your chosen platform brings confidence.

❐ Large brands and companies should investigate worldwide social media data and select multiple platforms with the most users.

❐ Independent contractors, influencers, brand advocates, and small businesses should select platforms that have the most users to form the greatest relationships in the shortest time.

❐ Independent contractors, influencers, brand advocates, and small businesses should use more than one platform only if they already use a secondary platform for personal reasons.

❐ Take the time to learn the ins and outs of your chosen platform. Look for free tutorials from the platform creators.

❐ Select a platform that best allows you to embrace the 4Cs of Conversation, Community, Connection, and Communication.

*Looking ahead:* With social media, it's tempting to present images and ideas about ourselves and our business that simply aren't true. If you choose integrity as the currency of your relationships, the loyalty you receive back is priceless. With great business power comes great responsibility. In the next chapter, Compliance, we take a look at what you can and cannot—and what you should and should not—post about your business online.

# CHAPTER SIX

## Compliance

WHEN IT COMES to the idea of compliance, we could have two different —but equally crucial—discussions.

One discussion relates to product categories or industries. Guidelines for these are specific and exhaustive. For example, the wellness and nutritional supplement category, which comprises roughly 36% of the $34 billion direct-sales industry in the US[5], has rules about claims related to health that have different nuances than cosmetics. Compliance in the energy company space has unique and separate guidelines from the housewares or telecommunication or prepaid legal services categories. This chapter does not cover discussions related to categories or industries—the topic is simply too vast—but that doesn't lessen its importance. Before you embark on a business in any category, research compliance rules in your industry.

This chapter focuses on brand advocates, the heart of Predictive Social Media, and what compliance means for this public-facing side of your business.

## BUILDING OUT A SYSTEM, IN ORDER

To be successful with Predictive Social Media, it's important to know the journey's order: customer, customer referrer, brand advocate.

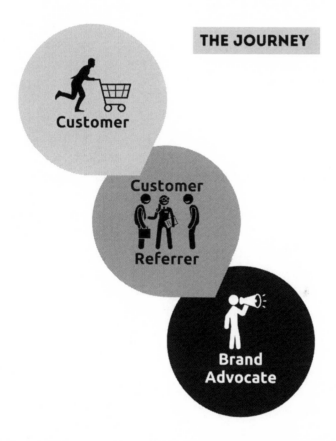

**THE JOURNEY**

Customer

Customer Referrer

Brand Advocate

The first stage, *customer*, is all about acquiring personal customers using the 7Cs. You're making connections and establishing relationships so that when friends have a life event that opens them up to your product or service, they will come to you.

At some point, however, despite the system's guarantee that you'll never run out of people to talk to, there are only so many customers you can realistically obtain. Limitations on your time plateau your business' growth. A strong customer referral program expands that reach exponentially. Now, instead of hundreds of new customers per month, you're acquiring thousands through all of your customer's friends in exchange for a discount on your product or service. This second level of participant, *customer referrer*, is how you'll snowball your numbers.

Your business may have an existing customer referral program. Perhaps it's parked on your website but hardly anyone takes advantage of it. It doesn't work. It falls flat because there are no brand advocates to encourage customers to refer friends. These programs shift the burden to the customer to be proactive and refer—essentially placing them in the role of brand advocate—when the customer may not desire to engage at that level and workload.

Predictive Social Media customer referrals work because brand advocates drive customers to refer. Customers hand referrals over to brand advocates, and brand advocates do the heavy lifting. The 7Cs, along with the power and reach of social media, is a referral program accelerant.

Out of your customer referrals program, an incredibly small and talented group will emerge. These individuals become your *brand advocates*.

Brand advocates of all categories have an equal opportunity to destroy a business if they don't follow compliance rules. Exposure risks to companies via brand advocates is huge. Let's ensure that doesn't happen.

Irrespective of where your business falls on the continuum of this system, understanding the fundamentals of compliance protects you and your business *before* you hang your best self out on social media.

Compliance sounds like an excuse to take a nap or for business lawyers to justify their hourly wage. Forgive me when I belabor the importance of this C. You might do all the other Cs in the system correctly, but what will it matter if it gets you into legal hot water?

## CLAIMS

A claim is a statement someone makes as truth, usually without reinforcing proof. Because of this lack of evidence, claims are easily refuted. Counter arguments on social media are a sport for some. Smart business owners know product, income, and lifestyle claims can be dangerous territory, for legalities as well as for optics.

### Express and Implied Claims

An express claim is literally made in the ad [post]. For example, "ABC Mouthwash prevents colds" is an express claim that the product will prevent colds. An implied claim is one made indirectly or by inference. "ABC Mouthwash kills the germs that cause colds" contains an implied claim that the product will prevent colds. Although the ad [post] doesn't literally say that the product prevents colds, it would be reasonable for a consumer to conclude from the statement "kills the germs that cause colds" that the product will prevent colds. Under the law, advertisers [and brand advocates] must have proof to back up express and implied claims that consumers take from an ad [post].

–FTC.gov[6]

## PRODUCT OR SERVICE CLAIMS

Compliance in terms of a product falls into two categories: value and claims.

Value is the stand-alone worth of the product—a fair exchange of goods or services for the money used to purchase it. Simplified, it's the question, *Would I buy this product?* If the product is a face cream that occupies a big-box-store shelf but is priced 500X higher than all of its competition on the shelf beside it, the value isn't there.

Product claims depend on the industry. For example, a statement that a nutritional drink reduces inflammation can be illegal. You cannot make a statement—express or implied—that your health supplement cures, treats, or heals. **Just because it's true doesn't mean you can say it.** To do otherwise turns the product into a drug when it has not gone through your country's health regulatory agency. Companies are required to meet confident, reliable, scientific, and evidentiary standards to make such claims and often have lab-supported results from reputable institutions. Instead of chancing illegal product claims, direct interested parties to company-issued literature.

## INCOME CLAIMS

As a successful brand advocate, you'll be acquiring many customers. Every now and then, you'll come across someone who secures great customer referrals. This happens about one or two times out of every one-hundred customers. Maybe that someone loves the discounts your company gives on products or enjoys some other perk to refer customers to you. These shining stars are similar to you as a brand advocate: they have the skillset required to be an entrepreneur and they exhibit drive and ambition. They are elevated customers in every way.

In an ideal world, companies with brand advocate programs *should* pay the vast majority of commissions to the individual who secured the customer. The remainder of the commission should be allocated in a way that reenforces team cooperation and team sharing of the reward. Although generous, there is a potential pitfall to incentivization at this level. Brand advocates can be tempted into posting or messaging people in ways that cross the compliance line with respect to income claims.

Let's say, as a brand advocate, you're making $10,000 per month. You cannot post your income, expressly or indirectly, on social media. Others don't have your skillset or expertise. They may lack your intensity or a thousand other variables that allow you to be successful when others sharing the same product or service are not. You cannot guarantee anyone else's income, so don't do it.

If you use my system properly, you'll never feel the need to post about your income. The majority of people who'll read your post and those who are customers don't care about your income and will view income posts as bragging. Additionally, people who reach this level of relationship with you, the ones who are motivated to take that next step into brand advocacy, are already believers in the product or service. Flaunting how much money you make won't change that, and it may turn them off.

## LIFESTYLE CLAIMS

Maybe you think it's in poor taste to post about money, but you love making lifestyle posts. Posts that show you driving a nice car, poised on the balcony of an exclusive country club, or wearing $5,000 shoes and directly attributing your ability to afford these things to your jackpot business—express or implied—is as harmful and illegal as income claims. You're communicating to others that they, too, can live the lifestyle you enjoy if they become a fellow brand advocate; yet, again, there are no guarantees. Remember, a thousand variables.

A tiny fraction of your business—those rock stars who would make excellent brand advocates—are smart. They're already diehard customers, they know how the product or service works, they conduct themselves as professionals, and they've proven that they have what it takes to build a business because they've already referred many people. If you talk to them about money or lifestyle, you will turn them off. Instead, say, "You love this product. You have incredible skills. You are already telling others about the product. Are you interested in making money with this product?" Almost always, they'll say yes because they're already energized.

Product, income, and lifestyle claims are problematic and might trigger the Federal Trade Commission (FTC) or the Food and Drug Administration (FDA) in the US, or the government equivalent in your country, to look closer at your business. Companies can buffer a bit of scrutiny by providing a disclaimer—basically a legal statement during the first nine to twelve months of your business' operation that details how there are no guarantees with relation to the product or service. In recent years, simple and blanket statements such as "results may vary" have become meaningless and frowned-upon. A good, substantial disclaimer should be drawn up by a lawyer in your industry.

After the initial nine to twelve-month grace period of your business' inception, your business will find it advantageous to prepare a legal document of disclosure. With relation to income, these disclosures often detail the number of brand advocates, their titles within the company, how much the company invested to get those individuals to that level of income, and the income ranges enjoyed by brand advocates.

A day may come when you are having a conversation with one of these potential brand advocates and you are asked a pointed question regarding your income. You *must* honor compliance, even in these one-on-one conversations.

However, if you are using the system correctly, you're not talking about an opportunity. Your conversation will always revolve around the product or service. Let's work through a potential scenario.

Your star customer and potential brand advocate—let's call her Nicole—asks, "Can you really make money on this?"

You answer, "Do you believe in this product?"

"Of course, I do."

"And you're enjoying the perk of getting it for free right now?"

"Yes."

"Do you think others would like to enjoy the benefit the way you do?"

"Sure."

"Do you believe others who love the product the way you do might begin to refer you to others?"

"Yes."

"How much money do you want to make?"

At this point, Nicole might say, "My goal is to make five thousand dollars a month."

Reason kicks in for you. You respond, "Let's keep the number to a good starting point. How about five hundred dollars per month?"

"Okay."

"Let's talk about what you'll need to do in order to create five hundred dollars per month. You'll need five customers whose average order is one hundred dollars . . ."

Do you see how redirecting the discussion back to the product and empowering Nicole's drive to succeed allowed you to help her through consideration while also respecting compliance? Steer away from talking about your income and you'll always be compliant.

If your friend persists—some people are numbers people—refer her to the company's income disclosure statement.

Later, in the Communication section, we'll discuss more about the kind of posts that are not only compliant but effective. If you post updates on your life—your wins and struggles—each week, your social media friends become a part of that narrative and doors will open to discuss your product or service.

One of my dear friends, Donna Marie Serritella, a 27-year veteran in direct-sales compliance, eloquently states, "There are a million mistakes a business can make, but if you have integrity, you'll build a brand advocate program with integrity. If you have compassion, you'll build a brand advocate program with compassion. Make sure you know your culture before you start because that's what you're going to build." She goes on to underscore the consequences of non-compliance. "When a business doesn't comply with rules, that business is setting itself up for future problems. Non-compliance can cause the owner to lose the business."

When done right, Predictive Social Media eliminates the stress of what you should post. Words become intuitive. You'll create the right culture. Compliance is important, but don't let adherence to it drive fears.

All size businesses should research the dos and don'ts in their specific industry and create an at-a-glance social media plan for brand advocates. In addition to the standard topics of platforms and goals and accountability and oversight, issues of compliance related to language used and legality ensures that brand advocates always represent the business in the best possible light.

## PREDICTIVE CHECKLIST: COMPLIANCE

❐ The Predictive Social Media journey happens in the right order: customer, customer referrer, brand advocate.

❐ If you're using the system the right way, you'll never post income or lifestyle claims.

❐ Product, income, and lifestyle claims are problematic and might trigger the government oversight agencies in your country to look closer at your business.

❐ Posting updates on your life, wins and challenges, builds friendships that open the door to discussing your product or service.

❐ All size businesses should research the dos and don'ts in their specific industry and create an at-a-glance social media plan for their brand advocates.

---

*Looking ahead:* In the first of the foundational Cs of Predictive Social Media—Conversation—we'll look at the art of discourse. Honest discussions inside social media help forge new relationships and strengthen existing friendships. I'll offer scripts for those who struggle in the area of conversation, to get you thinking in the right direction, but by the end of the chapter, you'll be adapting the words to come from a true place that touches on your core values. You'll also learn the all-important 90-day test.

# CHAPTER SEVEN

## Conversation

JULIAN IS A MULTI-BILLIONAIRE.

Let that sink in for a moment. I sure had to. Multi. Billionaire. I'm not one to become hypnotized by the wealth of others, but Julian has the kind of wealth that affords him a chance to extract a spare body part and ship it into space, purely for bragging rights. Despite assurances from our mutual acquaintance—"You'll love him, he's taken twelve of his companies to a billion in sales, his entrepreneurial track record is unprecedented!"—I wasn't as impressed as I might have been because life had just dealt me one of those hands that buckles the knees and rides the chest like a lead apron.

My mom was close to dying. At sixty-five pounds, in a medically induced coma for three months, machines ate and breathed and sustained for her. I signed papers no son should have to sign and paced the hospital wing, acquainting myself with the reality of losing my best friend. The fear and vulnerability I carried with me into my meeting with Julian made me a bit reckless, fearless, honest in a way that only the reminder of impending death can. My priorities had shifted. The things in life I believed to be the Holy Grail didn't hold up anymore.

Part of me knew Julian was open to what I had to say. Our thirty-minute scheduled phone conversation had turned into a two-and-a-half-hour question and answer session about my social media expertise. I worried I had dominated the call, but Julian kept asking questions until he said, "How soon can you get here?"

I thought of my mom. If she knew a guy who had the resources to ship body parts into space for sport wanted to talk to her son, she would tell me to go. Two hours. Then I'd be back on a plane and at her bedside before nightfall.

"Day after tomorrow," I said.

Working with a billionaire was a dream come true. I had realized my own echelon of success—at the time, hundreds of millions in sales for my clients—but I still believed that to change the world, one needed the kind of gravity that only wealth brings.

Two hours into the scheduled two-hour meeting, Julian asked, "Jim, what do you think about network marketing?"

Old Jim might have sugar-coated my disillusionment. The Jim who needed to get back to his dying mom shot straight. "May I speak freely?"

Julian leaned forward, his suit cuffs hiked back. A shiny watch that probably told him the optimum time to hydrate based on biofeedback through his skin stood out in sharp relief to his Monaco tan. "Yes. That's what I want."

"Welcome kits are a total rip-off. I don't know why you're doing them."

He blinked. Once, maybe twice. "Would you excuse me?"

Julian exited the room. I envisioned him calling security. Instead, he called his entire team into the room.

"Tell them what you told me," prompted Julian.

Before, I was reckless, fearless, honest. Surrounded by seven of the most profitable executives in business, I felt like that kid taking out the trash in a burger drive-thru line all those years ago. Julian nodded at me as if to say, *It's okay*. I repeated what I had told Julian.

"Kits should be optional, or at least pack your kits with product so distributors have samples to share with friends and family the day they enroll."

I then double and triple-stacked my opinions.

"Compensation plans should be based on customers, not distributors. It's the only way to attract distributors who genuinely care about the products and will promote them forever."

"There are too many hoops to jump through to get paid as a distributor. Keep it simple. Pay a distributor well if they get customers. Or pay well if they decide to build a team. Don't force people to do one over the other. Not everyone wants to build a team."

"You're traditional network marketing. You're not building a company based on today's environment. Younger generations primarily build their business using social media. People aged thirty-seven to their mid-forties spend most of their time using social media. Even the mid-forties and up crowd is putting in more time on social media. You're forcing everyone to do home parties and making everyone feel like there's no other way to build their business. That just isn't true."

Two hours turned to eight. Take-out containers filled with food whose names I couldn't pronounce crowded the table. At one point, I argued with the CEO of one of the top nutritional supplement companies in network marketing.

Julian ate it up. Biggest grin in the room. Getting on into the evening, he paced laps around the runway-length table and told his team they had failed the people—that this, what I was saying, was what they had been missing. Maybe not the coziest path to bonding, but I had earned the team's respect with a persuasive and passionate debate on all the ways network marketing must change to move forward.

Finally, Julian turned to me and asked, "Jim, what do you want? What do you really want?"

Aside from a Bugatti for a day? My mother to live to see my son grow up? Julian's question had goals written all over it. Realistic, reaching goals.

"I want to change the world," I said. "But people tend to do their version of my social media system. They never realize the success they could have because they don't implement it the way it's taught."

Julian stopped pacing, tightened his stare, and punched the table.

Eight of us scrambled out of our skin.

"Jim, don't you ever say you can't change the world. You can, and you will, if you try."

Julian was personally affronted that I might give up my goal so easily. His outburst was a shade of passion, not anger. He, too, had risen from nothing. Julian once witnessed a robbery and chased the thief eight city blocks to get back what rightfully belonged to a corner grocery store, simply because it was the right thing to do. An unwavering moral compass charters his every decision. He is prosperous because he does what is right, not what impresses people.

This encounter with Julian was one of the most enlightening conversations I've had in my life. From that moment on, I stopped second-guessing myself. I refused to waver from my ideal to change the world. A two-hour exchange had quadrupled in length because a group of diverse people engaged in a spirited and honest exchange of ideas about a topic that ignited a common fire.

In the end, Julian shut down his network marketing arm and restructured his company to move closer to the brand advocate model, something we discussed that fateful day. Prior to our meeting, most of the distributors in his company were in the company because of opportunity. Most believed that if a billionaire was behind the company, they would get rich. Most touted Julian's name all over the internet and social media as the reason to join. The product was an afterthought, at best. This misguided tactic upset Julian. He never wanted the business to be about him. Always, he wanted his products to be at the forefront of the company.

The few distributors who shared Julian's vision and who were there for the right reasons fought so much blowback and negativity from the majority, Julian had no choice but to restructure. Julian believes that the best path to building a huge business is to get customers excited about his products then have customers spread the word to their friends via social media. His new structure reflects this philosophy. This philosophy is what you are learning by using my Predictive Social Media system.

---

The Conversation portion of Predictive Social Media is all about how to have authentic and powerful discussions about your personal and business life to your social media friends, both existing and new.

Entrepreneurs and business owners want to have real conversations with those who might be interested in their product or service. It's not always easy. Maybe you have limited time to build your business, so making phone calls feels tedious. Maybe sending emails isn't giving you the results you seek. You now have a solution. By utilizing the power of social media, your ability to have real conversations with others becomes second-nature. Platforms allow you to know when people have seen your messages, make HD audio or video calls anywhere in the world, snap photos, shoot videos, chat with people in a group setting, record voice messages, and so much more.

Social media makes having conversations with potential customers and brand advocates, one-on-one or in a group setting, easy.

## CONVERSATION IN A SOCIAL MEDIA-DRIVEN WORLD

Face to face is still productive, and you should meet people in person as often as possible. Via social media, however, you can have a heart-to-heart video chat with anyone on the planet. Mind-blowing when you think about it, right? Plus, the interaction happens faster because you didn't have to first align crazy scheduling conflicts and travel.

Messaging also became a lifesaver. When all else fails, you can quickly send messages inside social media to communicate with friends in a one-on-one, intimate setting.

Today, three-way phone calls happen in social media messages. Everyone responds when they are available, not when schedules align (which may be never).

The same conversation principles of business that worked for peddlers hawking wares from their carts hundreds of years ago, the same principles that have worked for me for over two decades, still work today. People hearing your voice and seeing your facial expressions as you enthusiastically talk about a product or service that changed your life is the pulse of a successful business. Social media reaches this pulse better than any other form of technology today. When done right, social media is the new standard of authentic conversation—perhaps more powerful than meeting people in person because time is flexible and relationships develop at a pace that's favorable to all parties instead of forced at a specific time and location.

# CONVERSATION TIPS

Old and new friendships benefit from quality interaction. Here are some of my best tips to ensure conversations turn into lasting relationships.

### NEVER PREJUDGE

In my early 20s, I was an independent contractor for Cutco. You may have heard of this company. Their scissors cut through a penny. While there are, arguably, few things more impressive to a woman than scissors with the capacity to sever anything, I found myself in a Cutco knife-selling class, trying to do just that—impress a woman.

Tess didn't need the class. Really, she could sell knives to a samurai just by walking in a room. She wore a sweater over an untucked, button-down shirt, crisp sleeves rolled just-so, with a contrasting scarf casually looped around her neck. Her blond hair was tied up in loose waves, her deck shoes coordinated perfectly with the rest of her ensemble, and her plaid cross-bag held books and glasses that made her look straight out of a New England boarding school. I believed we might have commonalities because we both dressed preppy. Truthfully, I would have bought knives from her for simply glancing my direction, but a group of us decided to hang out after class and I invited her along. Tess came, and we had a blast. Though we didn't exchange phone numbers, I learned through the Cutco grapevine that she was attending a local fair the next weekend.

My plan to casually run into her at the fair died the moment I rounded a funnel cake stand. Tess wore black leather, head to spiked boots, and milled around neck-tattoo guys who looked like cautionary steroid tales. One look at my flipped-up, Polo-collared reflection in the fun-house mirror, and I headed home. I learned from friends in town that biker Tess was the true Tess. Had I seen her for the first time at the fair, I might have prejudged her. Motorcycles and the lifestyle that accompanies them aren't my thing, though I have many friends who have since tried to change my mind. Because I initially met Tess in an environment comfortable to me, an environment to which she had adapted to fit in, I asked her to hang out.

Never prejudge. Tess conformed to her surroundings. How many other social media friends of yours do the same? People are exquisitely complex, with diverse backgrounds and varied life experiences. Most people are a potential customer for your business, even if they may not seem so at first glance. All it takes is one small conversation to open acquaintances up to trying a product or service. Prejudgment causes us to miss out on life's opportunities.

## INTERPERSONAL SKILLS

My ability to talk to people has ebbed and flowed throughout my life. At times, I could engage anyone about anything. Other times, I was in relationships that were unhealthy for me and suppressed my outgoing nature. One season I was confident and the next season something would happen to tap back into my old insecurities. So, at a time when I had lost my ability to speak to strangers without fear, I took a summer job selling newspapers for a local company in front of a Walmart.

The experience was a mixed bag of outcomes. I had zero passion for selling this newspaper. I didn't care if people read it or not. But I focused on my objective: fearlessness when talking to strangers. After a few weeks, I had recaptured my interpersonal skills and sold a record number of subscriptions. I attribute this shift to two factors.

First, face-to-face selling is the most intimidating transaction in all of business. Rejection can be brisk and harsh. But face to face is also exhilarating. Success feeds upon the positive encounters that have come before.

Second, in that little enterprise outside the store, I had no one else on whom I could rely. I was an island, and islands get lonely. Why not talk to potential customers?

**You must talk to people. Speak up. Remember, the least amount of words possible to generate excitement in others to purchase your product or service is the most effective.**

## PEOPLE SKILLS

Back in 2001, I met a guy on Yahoo Chat named Ken. He suggested I use his business partner in India to set up a tech system I wanted to use to grow my business. Remember Naveen from my India story? This was my first contact with him.

Naveen quoted me a cost of $5,000 and a timeframe of four months. Two other estimates came in at $50,000 and $100,000, both with longer timeframes and additional hourly programming rates. Right about now, you're likely thinking what I was thinking: five grand sounded too good to be true, and anyone found on Yahoo Chat had the potential to be sketchy. I chose middle of the road, a decision I came to regret. Countless delays and an hourly rate that bled my funds dry left me with a broken infrastructure and enough software glitches to summon tears. Masculine tears.

I called Naveen. An eight-thousand-mile conversation couldn't mask the desperation in my tone. Naveen agreed to build the system and program for free. In return, he recouped his money by charging my brand advocates a monthly fee to access the system. He finished the work in three months, and it was perfection—no bugs, no glitches, no hassle. At this point, I would have married Naveen, but I settled for referring him to everyone I knew, without a thought to compensation. Naveen is brilliant at tech but needed help with business. We became good friends and partners in building a social network.

Ken believed in Naveen, but I didn't have enough of a trust component in Ken to take that original leap. When it came time for me to refer others to Naveen, they trusted me because I left no question in their minds that Naveen was the best. I was passionate about his knowledge, his work ethic, and his trustworthiness. I believed in Naveen before promoting his services to others. Naveen's tech business soared.

When people tell you about a product or service they love because they believe it will help you, too, it's selling. In essence, everyone sells. **To overcome that fear of selling, think of your business as a way to help people make the same difference in their lives that the product or service made in your life.**

In simple terms, people skills mean others genuinely like you. Your interactions are effortless. People are attracted to your companionship and like and trust you without much effort.

People skills can be improved if you're willing to be honest with yourself. What aspects of your interactions turn people off? What critiques have you heard in the past that made you defensive or unwilling to accept? If you struggle with self-assessment, ask someone whose honest opinion matters to you—a mentor, a supervisor, a coworker who has great rapport with everyone, a friend who always shoots things straight. Your business—and you—are worth a few moments of vulnerability.

## REAL FRIENDS

Nolan is a pool shark. On a mini-vacation one weekend, he challenged me to best of three. Best of three ballooned to best of 21 because I am so awful at the game. My clumsiness, however, was the greatest fortune of that weekend. Not only did it afford me the chance to get to know a true person who is inquisitive and always thinking outside the box, Nolan received advice on ways to improve his social media experience. At one point, I realized that Nolan was purposely underplaying to prolong our time together. I was training him in an environment where he felt comfortable, in a place he loved.

Traditional business theory would tell you this scenario is a mistake, that meeting a prospective buyer or customer on your terms gives you the selling advantage. This mindset is counterproductive to building real relationships. People who are in a comfortable environment are more open, more honest, more receptive to things that might be beyond their understanding. **Think of social media as the pool hall of business. You meet people in their environment, surrounded by the comfort of their friends and family. Take up residence in that zone first, as a trusted friend, and watch your business flourish.**

Nolan was already my friend. We had history, so being real with him was easy. When you're in the initial stages of a relationship, being a real friend means making overtures until you build a history.

Victoria sent me a friend request, along with a message: *Hey Jim! Love to stay in touch. Looks like we have similar hobbies.*

I replied, *Nice to meet you. I checked out your profile. Looks like we have* more than 40 mutual friends, as well. I'd love to hear why you decided to reach out to me. Looking forward to hearing from you soon.

Victoria wrote, *That was a fast reply! Social media suggested we should be friends. Looks like we are both entrepreneurs, so I thought why not? It looks like you've done well growing business on social media. I've been an entrepreneur for the last 5 years. Would love to stay in touch!*

We went back and forth a few more times until I felt comfortable that she wanted to be a real friend. Friend request accepted.

How should you handle friend requests from people you don't know? Treat a new friend request the same way you treat a person you meet outside of social media who wants to be your friend. On social media, go to the person's profile. What does the profile tell you? Sometimes you can tell the profile is fake. Other times, you know it's real because of the mutual friends, thoughtful posts, and comments from real friends.

Next, reply back to your new friend and start a one-one-one conversation. Continue the chat until you feel comfortable this person wants to be your real friend. Focus on the relationship. **Don't discuss your business unless this person asks.** Once you feel comfortable knowing this person's motive, accept or decline the friend request.

Damian was the opposite of Victoria. Damian's profile was largely empty. He had two pictures and little banter on his posts. We did not have mutual friends. I sent him a private message similar to Victoria. He never responded. Result? I declined his friend request.

Being a real friend is a gift you give someone. When that gift is reciprocated, it can feel like climbing inside a car warmed by the sun on a chilly day. Isn't that what you hope your customer feels about your product or service? That warmth begins with you.

## LIFE EXPERIENCES

My friend, Jackie, is exceptional at entrepreneurship. I asked her to look at Predictive Social Media because it might help her with her business. She said, "No thanks, Jim, but I appreciate you asking."

Does she need my system? Definitely. Does she think she needs my system? Definitely not. We have liked and commented on each other's posts and wished each other happy birthday for years. Jackie also trusts me. She knows I am passionate about social media and have the credibility to back up what I teach. Though I may inspire her, she has not yet had a life experience to make her think she needs my system.

A life experience is a traumatic event that raises awareness about something a person needs to improve. Unless the event triggers distress, most people won't change. This desire for change causes a person to seek out products or services that offer helpful solutions to the challenge. If you have established your business as that solution and you've grown the relationship, a beautiful moment of unity with the capacity for human impact happens.

People usually get excited to purchase your product or service for one of two life experience reasons.

- **Emotional Impact**: A customer anticipates feeling better by consuming your product or experiencing your service. This reason may be tied to the customer's core values.
- **Features**: Definitive reasons why your product or service brings value to someone's life. Often, these are qualities that set your product or service apart from the competition.

Emotional impact and features apply to every product and service. Discover your product or service's emotional impact and features that move people to action. Once you've discovered these, you'll be better equipped to communicate effectively with your friends about your business. Knowing the decision-making drives for your customers will help you zero in on ideal customers.

## BE THE REAL YOU

Early in my entrepreneur life, my friends thought it would be best if I got a local job. I recall my closest high school friends taking me out for a drink at a pub a couple of years after high school graduation. They sat me down for the big talk.

"Jim, you're an awesome guy, but you're shooting too big. We believe in you, but you're not going to make it. People like us don't get rich, and we don't change the world. Rich people change the world."

No small surprise: this non-truth played in my head for years, until Julian punched the desk and knocked it out of me.

A few drinks later, the message shifted. "Stay in town with us. We can go out on the weekends. Have fun. Get a good job here. Go to college down the road. By the time you get out of college, you can be bringing in $30,000 a year then maybe work your way up to $100,000 a year someday."

I had enough. Drinks. Skewed philosophies. Negativity.

"Listen, guys," I said. "I love you. I have no idea how I am going to do it. I don't expect you to believe in me. But I believe in me. I know I can change the world. I know I can change *my* world. I'll fail a thousand times, but I'll also succeed. I don't care about a job or what you guys say is job security. I also don't believe your rants about rich people. I deserve a great life, and so do all of you. Come with me. Let's do it together."

They looked at me as if I had recited the Declaration of Independence backwards. We left that night in silence. I went my way; they went their way. It's been over twenty years since that night. I haven't had a job since. I changed my world. More importantly, I changed the worlds of many others.

How should you handle negativity or off-the-wall responses when doing Conversation in social media?

Be you. Speak from the heart and show confidence in your business. Use your product or service daily. You know it works; therefore, it will work for others.

I sent Cheryl a friend request on social media. She did not accept my friend request. Instead, she sent me a message on social media. The message read, *Hi, Jim. I can't accept your friend request. I'm sorry. I'm happily married.*

Huh? I was speechless. I replied, *Hi, Cheryl. I'm glad you're happily married, as well. Did you happen to read my message that went along with my friend request? Please check it out. If you feel we could be friends, I'd love to hear back from you.*

She responded, *I'm sorry, Jim. Please stop contacting me. I don't have time to check out your message. Again, I'm married. This just isn't right.*

I responded, *Be well, Cheryl.*

Sometimes things won't make sense. As Bruce Lee once said, "Honestly express yourself." You can't go wrong if you stay true to the real you.

## DON'T BE AGGRESSIVE

Maddie calls once a year with a new product for me to try. Each phone call is filled with excitement and usually goes like this: "Hey Jim! It's Maddie. Listen, I found a product that is going to change your life. It did for me. Can I tell you about it?"

After she's finished talking, I usually say, "Hey Maddie. What happened to the last product or the product before that? You were as excited about those products, and now you're no longer promoting them. It makes me wonder if this product you're telling me about is really any good." It's hard for me to listen to Maddie because this has been going on for fifteen years.

How do you contact friends if you were already too aggressive with them in the past?

Since building a relationship is key, it's best for you not to talk about your business on social media for thirty days. Consider it a reset. Focus on building relationships with all of your friends when you reach out to them on social media. If you are in business for the long haul, this is the way to go.

My other friend, Kathy, is the opposite of Maddie. Eighty percent of the time, Kathy talks to me as a friend. She reaches out to me from time to time on social media and asks how my family is doing, or if I'll be attending an upcoming event. We chat as friends. Every now and then, she reminds me about her business. I don't mind hearing about her business because I know she is my real friend. A day may come when I have a life experience and need a product or service like hers. I will order from her over anyone else because she cares about me as a person.

**If you've been aggressive in the past, reset. Focus on the relationship. Your business will always be there as long as the relationships with friends are meaningful.**

# STARTING CONVERSATIONS WITH NEW FRIENDS

If starting a conversation with people in person is difficult for you, you're not alone. Social media makes this ice-breaker easy. The pressure to respond when someone is looking at you, in person, can be intimidating. On social media, you can take your time and think about what you want to say by reviewing a person's profile. Let's break down how best to start a sincere dialog on social media.

New friends may accept your request but never see the message you sent along with the request. You'll know this on some platforms because a photo of your friend will display next to the message to indicate that person saw your message.

The best approach is to resend the original message within 24 hours of your new friend accepting your request, with one tweak. Start the message by saying, *Hey* (new friend)! *Not sure if you saw my original message from my friend request. Here it is again.* (insert the original message).

On some platforms, you'll notice that friends accept your friend request and see your message but fail to respond. People get distracted. Often, your new friend will welcome your response as a reminder.

The best approach in this case is to say, *Hey* (new friend)! *I noticed you saw my message, and I thank you for the new friendship. Looking forward to seeing your posts.*

If your new social media friend accepts your friend request and responds to your message, reply with, *Hey* (new friend)! *Thanks for accepting my friend request and responding to my message. I'm really excited to build a friendship with you.* Continue the interaction based on what your new friend says. Your objective is to have a real conversation.

If your new friend does not accept your friend request but reads your message and does not respond, try, *Hey* (new potential friend)! *I noticed you saw my message. I also sent you a friend request.* Then say something more substantial than you said in your original message.

Your new friend may respond to your message but not accept your friend request. In this case, respond with, *Hey* (new friend)! *Thanks for replying to my message. I sent you a friend request.* Continue the interaction based on what the person said in her last message. Speak from the heart and be yourself. If the connection is meant to be, your new friend will accept your request.

You're now starting conversations. When making decisions about how many times you should go back and forth with people or what should you say, put yourself in their shoes. How often would you want them to interact with you?

Social media makes starting conversations easy. Always try to reach out to new friends within 24-48 hours. Interact with new friends based on their last interaction with you. Whether your new friends have seen or not seen, and responded or not responded to your message request, each action deserves a unique reply. When starting the conversation, the most important piece of advice is simply to start.

## STARTING CONVERSATIONS WITH EXISTING FRIENDS

Starting a conversation with existing friends on social media is easier than connecting with new friends for the first time. The history is there. You have liked or commented on each other's posts, wished each other happy birthday, and interacted in other ways.

I hadn't spoken to Adam for six months. Adam is one of those cool dudes. He has travelled everywhere, knows everyone, listens to a wide range of music, and has a diverse group of friends. I visited him once, and it was a day to remember. In the morning, we hung out with a group of guys from Asia, talking about technology. In the afternoon, we chilled with a group from Europe and discussed meditation and yoga. That evening, we jammed out with a bunch of his friends at a back-in-the-woods type of outdoor concert.

I thought Adam and I were fantastic friends, so I reached out to him: *Hey Adam! How have you been? I found this shaving cream that makes my face look and feel fantastic. I've been using it for a few months, and it's all-natural. Can I send you a sample?*

He replied, *Nice to hear from you too.*

Ouch.

I hadn't spoken with Adam in six months. When I reached out to him, I focused on selling instead of reconnecting. In essence, my misguided message conveyed to Adam that he was not a friend but a means to a sale.

To remedy my mistake, I responded back right away and changed the subject. A month later, after a lot of rebuilding the relationship, Adam took a sample. He became a customer, as well. Adam could have totally blown me off, and I might have lost a friend. He gave me a second chance. You may not be so lucky.

Starting a conversation with existing social media friends happens when you visit the friend section on the platform of your choice.

The friend section is anywhere that displays all of your existing social media friends. Friends may be in order, based on your level of interaction. Sometimes, the default option is all friends; however, many platforms give you the option to sort friends based on searches, such as friends who attended the same school.

The group of friends that appear at the top of the default option are likely people with whom you recently spoke and enjoy the best relationships. You might find yourself talking about your business right away with top default friends. As you make your way down the list, you may need to focus on building the relationship before you discuss business. If the platform has a sorting process, lean into that feature, either default or self-created, and let that be your guide.

I hadn't spoken to Linda in more than three months. As much as I wanted to tell her about aromatherapy products I found and loved, I followed my system. I knew from her posts that Linda loved all things Hawaiian, and she used aromatherapy to help her capture that island spirit and de-stress. Imagine how hard it was for me to hold back until we reconnected.

I sent her a message and said, *Hey Linda! It's been quite a while since we last spoke. How have you been? I've seen some of your travel posts. Looks like you're seeing the country.*

She responded with, *Hey Jim! Long time, no hear. Life has been great! I'm traveling with the hubby, enjoying life. We are in retirement. I'm happy you said hi. We are off to the next spot. Chat soon!*

I wrote, *Looking forward to seeing your travel pictures. I'm doing a little traveling myself. Headed off to Colorado. Thanks for responding so fast. Take care!*

Two weeks later, Linda commented on one of my posts about the aromatherapy products and asked for a sample. She became a customer and, eventually, a brand advocate.

Had I contacted her with a business-first mindset, she may have thought of me as a salesman and not a friend. Because relationships are crucial to me, I focus first on building trust, second on business.

How many existing social media friends should you reach out to per day? I recommend a minimum of 10 and maximum of 30. Reach out to friends via your laptop or phone. It's fast and easy. In fact, once you get the hang of it, reaching out should only take you one minute per friend.

The reconnection, alone, feeds the soul.

## THE 90-DAY TEST

Scroll to your last conversation with your existing friend. Check the date stamp. How long has it been since you chatted with your existing friend?

**More than 90 days:** Think about friends outside of social media. If you haven't spoken to someone in three months, would you call your friend out of the blue and immediately start telling him about your business? Of course not. You would take the first fifteen minutes to catch up on life. Catching up on life inside of social media is reestablishing the relationship.

Send a message like, *Hey* (friend)*! It's been a while since we last chatted. How have you been?* Go back and forth two or three times, talking about life, not business. During the Communication portion of Predictive Social Media, your friend will learn more about your business, anyway. For most people, 80% of their social media friends will fall into this scenario. So, if you have 1,000 social media friends, 800 will receive this type of message.

**Less than 90 days:** Suppose you chatted with your friend a month ago about your children's basketball game and exchanged action photos. Sounds like you have a relationship. You might say, *Hey* (friend)*! I just wanted to reach out and let you know I've been using an eco-friendly line of cleaning products on my home, and they work wonders. They're pet-safe too.*

*I decided to share it with others to get free product. Would you be interested in trying a sample?*

What happened? You told your friend why you are sending the message. You shared your personal testimonial of your product. You also shared a product fact. It doesn't matter the product or service. Everyone has testimonials and facts to back up the quality of their product or service. You should also let your friend know why you are sharing the product or service. You are getting something if your friend purchases, so be transparent. Friends will appreciate it. Honesty helps friends become customers. This transparency also lets your friend know there is an opportunity to get something beyond a great product or service.

About 20% of your social media friends will fall into this group. Continuing the example in the previous section, this means you will have spoken to 200 of your social media friends in the past 90 days. Of these 200 friends, 80% of them will need to hear the type of message above. You can be direct with the other 20%, or 40 of the 200, because you know them on a more personal level. Likely, the enhanced knowledge you have of these 20% will help you understand how they might find interest in your business.

You might say, *Hey* (friend)*! I just wanted to reach out and let you know I've been using an eco-friendly line of cleaning products on my home, and they work wonders. They're pet-safe too. I decided to share it with others to get free product, and I know you've been looking for something like this for awhile. Would you have an interest in trying a sample?*

## CONVERSATION TIERS

If you are a brand advocate, there are four tiers of Conversation when it comes to telling your friend why you are reaching out. The conversation stays the same, but the end changes based on where you are in your brand advocate career.

**The first tier.** You want to get free product. Perhaps you'll say: *I like it so much, I decided to share it with others to get the product for free.*

**The second tier.** You want to make extra money. The conversation may sound like this: *I like it so much, I decided to share it with others to make some extra money. I already get the product for free.*

**The third tier.** You want to earn a part-time income. The conversation may include, *I like it so much, I decided to share it with others. I already get the product for free and earn extra money. I am trying to earn a part-time income now because I love the products so much.*

**The fourth tier.** You want to earn a full-time income. The conversation may end with, *I like it so much, I decided to share it with others. I already get the product for free and make a part-time income. I am trying to earn a full-time income now because I love the product so much.*

Focusing on the product but adding some form of these words, depending on the stage of your brand advocate career, can make a big difference in what materializes from these conversations.

What if your business is what some people consider a more difficult product or service to share with friends? Let's say you own a tax accounting business. Try, *Hey* (friend)*! I wanted to let you know I'm giving a 50% discount to all my social media friends who let me do their taxes next year* (why you are reaching out). *I've been able to save the average customer $6,700 on their taxes this year* (your product fact). *I'm passionate about taxes (I know weird), but I really love helping people.* (Your product testimonial). *Would you have an interest in learning more about how the 50% discount works?*

You don't have to mention you are going to get free product or earn money because this example is for a small business. The only people who need to talk free product or earn money as the example above are brand advocates.

# ORGANIZING CONVERSATIONS

As you reach out to your existing social media friends, each friend will be at a different stage of deciding to do business with you. To better serve your friend, you should know your friend's decision-making stage and sort accordingly.

Over the years, I've tried many different lists. The list organization is part of the formula you learned at the beginning of the book. Use paper or notebooks or find an app or software to help you stay organized. Here are the lists that work best within the system.

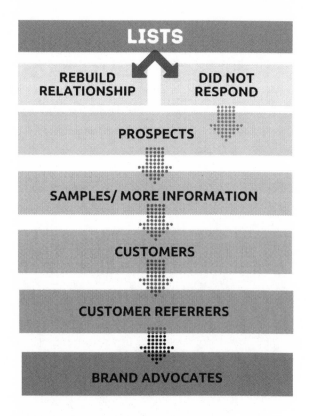

Initially, friends will go into one of two lists: **Did Not Respond** or **Rebuild Relationship**.

- **Did Not Respond:** All friends who did not go in the Rebuild Relationship list go into this list until your friends respond back to you. Once they respond back, put friends into a Prospects list.
- **Rebuild Relationship:** You haven't spoken to these people in 90 days. Your goal is to catch up on life, not discuss business.
- **Prospects:** As friends respond back—only those from the Did Not Respond list—they will say yes or no to your offer. Friends go into the Prospects list regardless of their answer. If friends took the time to respond to you, they are considered a prospect for your business, now or in the future. It means you have a relationship.
- **Samples/More Information:** As friends go through my system, you will send them samples or more information, as well as add them to your community. If friends are trying a sample or reviewing more information, put those friends in the Sample/More Information list. Do not remove them from the Prospect list. Now they are showing up in two lists. These are your hottest prospects—the ones most likely to do business with you.
- **Customers:** When a friend orders your product or service, put your friend in the Customer list. This allows you to stay in touch on a personal level with friends who use your product or service.
- **Brand Advocates:** When a friend shares your product or service with others and decides to become a brand advocate for your business, put this friend in your Brand Advocate list. This allows you to stay in touch on a personal level with friends who refer your business to others.

Starting the conversation with existing social media friends about your product or service is a continuation of open exchanges you should already be having. Discuss business only if you have a real relationship with your friends. Obey the 90-Day Test. Keep your business organized by using social media friend lists. When starting the conversation, remember that these people are already your friend for a reason.

## CONTINUING CONVERSATIONS WITH SOCIAL MEDIA FRIENDS

Continuing conversation is a back and forth melody between you and your friend. First and foremost, it's about nurturing a friendship. Secondary to that is figuring out if you inspire your friend with your business and if your friend has had a life experience so that he may benefit from your product or service.

While your exact conversation will and should be unique to the relationship you build with your friend, here is a mockup of how I might continue the dialog.

I send my friend, Tim, a message to check out the Predictive Social Media system. I spoke to Tim less than 90 days ago. He's had a life experience—maybe the birth of a child—so he's always looking for ways to grow his business. He likes me because we talk to each other as friends on social media, not just about business. He is inspired by me to grow his business on social media because I use my system with success.

I message, *Hey Tim! I wanted to let you know that I launched my predictive system that teaches people how to grow a successful business on social media using the power of relationships. As you know, I have perfected this process over the last 25 years. Would you like to check it out?*

Immediately, I put Tim on the **Did Not Respond** list as a starting point.

Tim responds, *Sure, Jim. I'd love to hear more.*

I move him to the **Prospect** List.

I say, *Excellent! May I add you to our community so you can get all the information you need? I will tag you in a short video so you can decide. Feel free to ask questions about the system and hear from others having success. You'll also make some great connections for your business. After you check out the community, check out this website* (website URL). *I promise no hype. I think you'll also love the irresistible offer that makes everyone comfortable in trying the system. I will follow up with you tomorrow.*

Tim says, *Okay.*

I move him on the **Sample/More Information** list while keeping him in the **Prospect** list, as well.

The next day, I send Tim a message that reads, *Hey Tim! I'm checking in with you. What did you like the most about the community or website?*

If Tim responds with positive words, immediately hop on the phone or a video call to continue the conversation. Why? The success of your business is about relationships. You can't build relationships if you only type to each other. Hearing someone's voice or—better yet— seeing someone's facial features allows your friend to be inspired by your passion for your business and builds strong relationship bonds. If your friend has already had a life experience, the phone or video call will move them forward as a customer or brand advocate.

Here is the message you can use to get Tim on the phone: *It sounds like you liked what you saw in the community and website. Let's jump on the phone or video call for only 10 minutes so I can answer your questions. I'd love to say hello, as well. I can call you right now.*

**TIPS FOR A SUCCESSFUL 10-MINUTE CALL**

- The first minute is rapport. Prior to the call, look at your friend's social media profile and find something of interest. "Hey! Thanks for taking 10 minutes with me. We can go longer if you want, but I value your time. Before we talk business, I noticed on your profile that you were at Bieber Park this past weekend. That's a beautiful place. Did you enjoy it?"
- The next eight minutes is answering questions. If you can't answer a question, do a three-way social media message with an experienced brand advocate in your business. "Well, regarding the system. What questions do you have?"
- The final minute is a call to action. "It looks like I answered all of your questions. Are you ready to get started? If not, what else do you need from me?"

What if Tim doesn't respond to my message that prompted me to ask him to connect on a phone or video call? Allow a week to pass then send Tim a message: *Hey Tim! It's been a week since we last spoke. What do you think of the community I added you to or website?*

If a week goes by with no response, send Tim another message: *Hey Tim! Two weeks ago, you expressed interest in my Predictive Social Media system. Are you still interested?*

If a third week goes by and you still haven't received a response, send a third message: *Hey Tim! I hope everything is okay. I haven't heard from you. Out of respect, I won't be sending you any more messages about my business. Just let me know if you change your mind. In the meantime, our friendship is the most important. See you around!*

At any time during the conversation after Tim is added to the community, Tim may reply with interest.

If you distribute product samples when a customer is interested, consider the following: sending a sample too early will result in 1 out of every 20 people becoming a customer. Send the sample *after* your friend expresses interest from the community and connects with you on the phone or video chat and you'll notice 1 out of every 5 people become a customer.

If your business has a brand advocate program, it's important that you ask Tim to be a brand advocate only after he has been a customer for a while and referred some people. Why? Your strongest brand advocates will be those who believe in the product or service. Think about it. If Tim really believes in your product, he'll easily share it with his social media friends. Set Tim up for success. Don't rush him to be a brand advocate because you are excited that he will make money. If he fails, he won't think fondly of you or your business. The only exception is if Tim has been a successful brand advocate in the past with other products and services. He knows the role and its expectations.

Continuing the conversation is a series of coordinated steps that helps your social media friends make an educated decision about doing business with you. **Follow up with friends once a week for three weeks after they express interest in your business. Most importantly, keep the friendship going. You never know when someone will be ready to purchase your product or service.**

I met Dr. Silva through a mutual friend while in college. Immediately, I loved that he was a medical doctor who embraced holistic ideas, slightly unusual for a man of his advanced age. He had a thriving practice and a mane of silver hair that gave me life goals. His three-bedroom boat floated in a Baltimore harbor.

Not long after introductions, Dr. Silva invited my business partner and me for a sailing weekend that coincided with Independence Day. His wife was gracious, his boat was unforgettable, and his genuine interest in our product ensured we never lacked for conversation. We dipped our toes into the ocean, watched fireworks on the horizon, and made memories. After a dream weekend, we parted with words of intent to remain in touch. I returned to my life in Rhode Island.

A week or so later, I left voicemail messages for Dr. Silva. Occasionally, he tagged me back in a voicemail message and apologized for not getting back to me in a timely way, but he still expressed an interest in my product. For months, we played message tag until all responses from him stopped. I thought he decided not to move forward with my product or my friendship. To be sure, I gave him one more courtesy call.

He didn't respond.

Half a year passed. I made my way through my six-month list—follow-up calls I made to everyone who said no or three-strikes-you're-out people from sixth months prior, usually to the exact date (I was organized).

Dr. Silva's name came up on my list. I was apprehensive. Did I say something to offend him? How could that summer sailing trip have been such a memorable weekend for me and absolutely forgettable to him? I dialed. To my surprise, his receptionist put the call through.

"Hey, Jim. What happened to you?" he said. "I was so interested in your product, and you dropped off the face of the Earth."

I couldn't believe it. My brain cycled back to how this could have happened. Soon after I put Dr. Silva into my six-month follow-up system, I bought a new voicemail machine because my old one erased messages at random. Driving back for a face to face in Maryland had never really been an option because I was a poor college student, and the brochures I sent, most likely, became a casualty of unwanted deliveries to an overly busy office.

Shortly after I had added him to that sixth-month follow-up list, Dr. Silva met someone who marketed the same product and purchased through him. It seemed a small price to pay for a lesson learned until I found out Dr. Silva was purchasing more than $5,000 per month to sell in his clinic. This revelation felt a little like getting clocked in the nose by the boom on a sailboat.

We stayed friends. He called me from time to time over the next year with questions since his purchase guy quit the business. I never earned a commission from his efforts because his sales rolled up to the person who introduced Dr. Silva's purchase guy to my company.

Had social media been a tool in my marketing arsenal back then, miscommunication between Dr. Silva and me would not have happened. Over those six months, videos and updates—directly or indirectly—would have reminded him about our conversations regarding the product. Heck, a photo of me playing with my dog and a caption about my new healthy lifestyle might have snagged his attention on a day he was ready to place an order.

On most platforms, date stamps allow you to see when messages were delivered. It may also show an icon of your friend and something beside it to indicate your friend saw the message.

How can this help your business? For starters, it's nice to know your messages won't be erased. You can follow up with your friends in a timely manner without coming across as pushy. If you follow up with someone before they have a chance to see your message, your friend might feel like you're being too aggressive.

The functionality of most platforms to review messages is a gift. Imagine that after an entire year of talking to a friend they are finally ready to look at your business. Social media allows you a chance to review an entire year's worth of conversation, use that history for a nostalgic chat, and grow the relationship while the potential for new business is there. Beats my old index-card system, for sure.

Social media lets you share photos and videos. Add drawings or text to personalize your photos. Sharing pictures or videos of your products or services along with supplemental information might help friends decide sooner rather than later.

Personality builds relationships. Stickers, like smiley faces and dancing gifs, are a great way to convey enthusiasm for your products or services.

These are some of the features social media offers to grow your business. Embrace your chosen platform's distinctive features. Anything that enhances lines of conversation ensures that my missed opportunity with Dr. Silva will not happen to you. By using the full array of features on your chosen social media platform, you'll be in a position to have a conversation as memorable as one on the sun-drenched deck of a sailboat.

## THE SPECIAL CASE OF BIRTHDAYS

Wishing someone a happy birthday is effortless on social media and a great conversation starter. Many platforms broadcast anniversary-in-business or anniversary-on-the-platform mini-occasions, as well. These milestones, however significant or minor, present an opportunity to revisit the friendship.

I wished Ann a happy birthday and included a message based on a recent post I had seen about her family. I hadn't spoken to Ann in about six months.

Her response read, *Thank you so much, my dear Jim. You took the time out of your busy schedule to wish good ol' me a happy birthday. Means a lot at my age. I turned 60 and feel younger than ever.* Ann continued with two more paragraphs of kind words and finished by asking me how my son and business were doing. She had been watching my posts all this time, never liking or commenting, yet she messaged me like a dear friend. The entire exchange happened because I took time to wish her a happy birthday.

On most platforms, you can send a birthday wish publicly or privately. Most people reach out publicly because it's easier and faster. I prefer reaching out to the birthday person privately so my sentiment doesn't get lost amongst all the other well-wishers. You're more likely to get a reply to a private happy birthday message, and the extra effort initiates a one-on-one conversation that grows the relationship.

Don't forget that birthday wishes go both ways—theirs and yours.

Here are some message ideas to get your creativity flowing.

- Sometimes, keep it short by messaging, *Happy Birthday!*
- Other times, add something valuable: *Happy Birthday! I really appreciate your friendship and all these years knowing each other.*
- Or make it personal by adding, *Happy Birthday! Not only do I appreciate our friendship, I love seeing your posts of your children. Your children are so happy and remind me of my little boy when he was the age of your children. Be well on this wonderful day.*

Above all, share the real you when wishing friends happy birthday.

If someone wishes you a happy birthday, wait one day before responding to give yourself time to collect as many birthday wishes as possible. Respond to direct messages first.

- Keep it simple by replying, *Thank you very much!*
- Start a conversation by saying, *Thank you very much! How have you been?*
- Create a conversation by making it personal: *Thank you very much! How have you been? I checked out your profile and loved your post yesterday about the turtle. Reminds me of the days I used to go to a lake as a teen.*
- Create a conversation geared toward business by saying, *Thank you very much! How have you been? I really appreciate us staying in touch.* (Then, only add the following if you have a real and recent relationship with your friend) *I was meaning to tell you that I've been using a new cosmetic line, and the autumn color palette is breathtaking. They're hypoallergenic too. I haven't broken out in months. It's mineral based, and I decided to start selling it so I could earn some free make up and a little extra money. Would you like some information about the line?*

Vary birthday wishes to others and your response when others wish you a happy birthday. Instead of always messaging, try some of the platform's other features to make a greater emotional connection than just words.

When you take the time to say happy birthday to a social media friend, it shows your friend that you care. Elevate yourself from the noise by sending private birthday wishes. Write a heartfelt message based on your relationship since your friend's last birthday. Happy birthday wishes enhance the relationship, which betters your chance of doing business with your friend.

## PREDICTIVE CHECKLIST: CONVERSATION

❐ Face to face is still powerful, and you should meet people in person as often as possible.

❐ Prejudgment will cause you to miss out on life and business opportunities.

❐ To overcome that fear of selling, think of your business as a way to help people make the same difference in their lives that the product or service made in your life.

❐ People skills can be improved if you're willing to be honest with yourself.

❐ Treat a new friend request the same way you would treat a person you met outside of social media who wanted to be your friend.

❐ A life experience is a traumatic event that raises awareness about something that a person needs to improve.

❐ Reach out to a minimum of ten and maximum of thirty existing social media friends per day.

❐ Use the 90-day test to decide if you should reach out to a friend regarding your business.

❐ Being transparent about where you are in your brand advocate career brings a level of respect to your business.

❐ Wishing someone a happy birthday is effortless on social media and a great conversation starter.

*Looking ahead:* **Few things in this life are more electric than a cluster of like-minded individuals, working in harmony toward a common goal—even if that goal is simply support.** That sense of belonging elevates Predictive Social Media beyond business and into matters of the human experience. In the next section on Community, you'll read about Jay, a man with a triumphant story about how Predictive Social Media became so much more than a way to accelerate business.

# CHAPTER EIGHT

## Community

JAY ANDERSON WAS ALWAYS an invincible guy. In high school and college, he excelled at cardio-heavy sports, such as cross-country, track, and basketball. His service nature and caring heart led him down a teaching path, and he found joy in working with young autistic men and women beginning their transition into adulthood. He enjoyed being a blessing to frightened parents. For Jay, assisting these challenged individuals with employment and independence was especially rewarding.

A parathyroid tumor in his forties began Jay on a downward spiral of health issues that eventually culminated in renal failure. At the same time he began attending seminars put on by the National Kidney Foundation called "The Big Ask," where guides instructed patients how to post on social media in a way that might encourage family, friends, and strangers to get screened for possible donation, Jay became acquainted with my social media system for business. While listening to my mentor calls, serendipity struck. Instead of a Go-Fund me account that centered exclusively on Jay, instead of one awkward ask, one time, the way the Foundation suggested, Jay saw my relationship-first system as a more sincere way to approach others about kidney donation—not just his, but on behalf of all patients hanging their future hopes on a donation.

Jay anchored his social media community with an inaugural post that was raw and vulnerable. "I bared my soul and asked for kind words and thoughts and prayers," he recalled. Jay then followed my systematic method of posting and engagements, placing particular importance on responding to every post message, every direct message, every interaction.

Soon, others began posting about health and life challenges, for them and for their loved ones. **Jay discovered that on his darkest days, when getting out of bed seemed an impossible task, his community needed his positivity and encouragement as much as he did.** Working through the system, Jay connected to friends with whom he'd lost contact, extended family, and strangers from around the world who reminded him of the universal nature of the human condition.

Jay has always been a spiritual man, but what struck him about my system was its capacity to elevate everyone in his community. Had his prayer group posted a sign at the church requesting prayers for Jay, the flow of connections would have gone one way and he might never have known and reciprocated the outpouring of support. **Predictive Social Media offered Jay the opportunity to give as much as he received, and the love multiplied.**

When Jay reflects on advice he'd give someone who finds this system compelling, he wants people to know that getting started can be the hardest part, but you don't have to be perfect. He certainly wasn't. Some days, low energy prevented him from implementing the system the way he wanted. Because the system is not only step-by-step in terms of follow up and interacting the right way but also comes from a place of genuineness, Jay was always able to pick up those connections when his disease allowed.

The rest of Jay's story has yet to be written. The average window for an O+ kidney donation is six to eight years without a direct-contact donor. He enjoys using my system to spread the word about paired donation and the special demands placed on the caregivers of those in renal failure. He believes the system aligns perfectly with the motto he lives by each day: go out and make a difference in your life for the ones you love.

Humans aren't meant to live in isolation. Research into the psychological value of community is extensive. Communities offer an emotional space to share experiences, openly bond with one another, offer support, and build relationships. Diverse communities are often rich in resources and skills, allowing everyone to bring a unique skillset to benefit the whole. Other components of a thriving community include shared purpose, the safe opportunity for people to be genuine, and empowerment in knowing that participation impacts the group.

While nothing quite beats face to face and physical contact—a handshake or a hug—virtual communities enjoy all of the above benefits with the added boost of a vast planet filled with people with whom we might not have otherwise encountered without technology. My father connects with fellow Dim Mak experts in the Far East. Jay unites people facing similar health challenges. I can be part of a group of entrepreneurs who don't judge me for breaking down every aspect of life into components. Even to build a delicious pastrami on rye, my brain gets excited at the process. Six Sigma for sandwiches, only I eat the data. While traveling, I'm also a sucker for finding the best places where locals hang out—hiking trails, pubs, you name it. My *local*, virtual communities span the globe.

Virtual business communities share all the benefits of personal communities with a few added considerations. As a community's leader or brand advocate tied to your product or service, you set the group's tone. **For everyone to feel like family, you must ensure a virtual space filled with respect and kindness. Boldly state your expectations when members opt in and hold members accountable for actions that do not support that mission.** From time to time, members may veer off the topic of your product or service—and that's okay—you're building relationships. Members should never be allowed to veer off into negativity, toxicity, or hostility.

## BENEFITS OF BUILDING A COMMUNITY ON SOCIAL MEDIA

Imagine walking into a room and hearing five hundred people rave about your business. Now imagine creating that room on social media. That is Community.

## GROWTH

Community happens when you're on—and off—social media. That means community advances and elevates your business during all hours of the day and night. When compared to more traditional product/service-to-customer environments aimed at growth, like one-way email funnels, communities enjoy exponential and expedited possibilities over options that depend on you to repeatedly initiate conversation.

## ENHANCED PURPOSE

A Community is essentially a group of people assisting each other toward a common goal. Sometimes, a community sprouts wings. People in groups tend to be more motivated, more creative, more productive. All that great fire has a spillover effect. Create the right culture and positivity in your community, and that feel-good notion will embrace your product or service and extend beyond what you might have envisioned. Think charity events, helping out a member fallen on hard times, and viral opportunities to share that positivity with the world beyond the group.

## RESPONSIVENESS

No matter how stellar your business offering, a day will come when a customer or brand advocate becomes frustrated with your product or service. No one is immune.

Many frustrations go unnoticed because people do not want to call the company to complain about something regarding a product or service. These people usually stop ordering the product or service and purchase from a competitor. Many times, the frustration is user error and has nothing to do with the product or service.

In a traditional business model, alleviating this frustration in real-time is impossible. Predictive Social Media helps you ease aggravations immediately. Addressing these individuals when their emotions are running high, giving them a safe place to ask questions, and providing a means to honestly express themselves is one of the greatest gifts your business can offer.

The community you build inside social media is that kind place.

In this cancel-culture era, when bad reviews can sink a business, I know this seems like opening the door to a dark and scary basement of public opinion. Stick with me. I have a lantern.

Your ideal community is hundreds—even thousands—of loyal customers and brand advocates who listen, relate, absorb, clarify misconceptions, and ease tensions about your product or service. Members know that they are free to voice concerns about a product or service. You become an open sounding board who has their best interests at heart and will do whatever it takes to serve them.

The result is nearly unshakeable social proof.

Surrounding your product or service with a strong, positive community also allows you to be proactive and minimize discontent before it takes root. Negative emotions have no time to fester because they are quickly addressed by the community. An offense *and* defense for disgruntled customers and brand advocates gives you the ultimate control over the narrative for your product or service.

Lucas was a friend of mine who hadn't been in Arizona long. He wasn't new to real estate, but he was new to the area. The guy worked to the bone, attending company training sessions, open houses, seminars, online workshops—anything and everything extra that might give him an advantage in a market in which he already felt behind.

Over lunch one day, he confessed to me that he hadn't made one sale in the six months he had been trying to establish himself in Phoenix.

"What advice do your coworkers have?" I asked.

"That's just it. I'm embarrassed to ask. I used to be the sales leader in my company back in Raleigh. It's like starting over twenty years ago."

I suggested he seek out a supportive community on social media— a network of like-minded, similarly-employed people who had experience in a climate and region and economy that was different from the one in which he had excelled back east.

"People are good, man," I said. "They want to help where they can. Human nature, karma, spiritual . . . whatever you want to call it."

The next month, Lucas and I met again for lunch. He already had two sales in the new month, and he directly attributed them to tips he learned from his new friends inside his social media community. Lucas prospered. The best part of his career, however, became the relationships he made from that network. He made it a point to log on each week to offer advice and lend support.

"I don't always have an easy solution," he told me. "Sometimes people just need a safe place to vent."

When you see a frustration post, comment to put that person at ease. Mine your early experiences with the product or service or business. Be specific and encouraging. Even if it's not your customer or a brand advocate with whom you work, you can make a difference in that person's experience. One day, one of your customers or brand advocates might post in frustration. In that event, you would want that person to feel the support that can only come from people who have had similar experiences.

## SOCIAL PROOF

The greatest risk in the above scenario is *not* that this individual may part ways with your product or service; the danger is that misinformation and discontent may influence others.

Suppose you drive past a seafood restaurant during open hours and the parking lot is empty. You assume the fish isn't fresh, the service is poor, or the atmosphere is dated or unclean.

Conversely, you drive past a custard shop. The crowd at the window is twenty people thick, and the drive-thru line wraps around the building. You assume the custard is spectacular. Why else would people be willing to take extra time out of their busy day for this particular custard stand?

Some call this *following the crowd*. Businesspeople know this as social proof. Second only to understanding the numbers, social proof is one of the most effective phenomena in business.

Social proof costs less than advertising and ensures that people are more loyal to your products and services. Word-of-mouth scales your business to unprecedented heights. Once upon a time, neighbors and friends shared these tidbits about your business over the back fence or a dinner party on Saturday night. Effective, but small.

> Social media allows people to broadcast their thoughts about your product or service out to a group of listeners as small as their following and, potentially, as numerous as millions if those thoughts go viral.

**If you structure your community correctly, negative social proof will be dealt with inside the group and positive social proof will thrive both inside and beyond the group.**

There are five types of social proof. Some are more impactful than others, and individuals respond differently to each type, depending on their core values. Of course, any of these can be used to paint your business with a negative brush, but let's focus on the positive bounce social proof provides.

## EXPERT

A credible expert or authority in an industry speaks highly about your product or service. If a dermatologist in the skincare industry mentions the benefits of your products, essentially an endorsement, you will likely see an increase in sales from anyone who trusts that doctor.

## CELEBRITY

A celebrity speaks highly about your product or service. One of our Predictive Social Media success stories is Dr. Roni DeLuz, two-time New York Times bestselling author and Hollywood's premier naturopathic doctor. Comedian and American television presenter Steve Harvey believes in Dr. Roni so much, he entrusts his life to her and says as much on social media. His celebrity status boosts her accomplishments; and, along with Predictive Social Media, Dr. Roni is enjoying peak enthusiasm about her teachings on social media.

## USER

Usually in the form of testimonials, a happy customer puts forth text, pictures, or videos praising your product or service. These can then be recycled as a social media post.

## WISDOM OF THE CROWD

This social proof speaks to the popularity of a product or service. Each time we see the term "most popular," our socialized brains want to know more about that product or service. We want to be in the know because it makes us feel informed.

## WISDOM OF FRIENDS

**Friends offer the most persuasive social proof. Wisdom of friends is one friend telling another friend about an experience they had with a product or service they cherish. In turn, this passion inspires their friends to want to try the product or service. Because we trust our friends, that trust transfers onto products and services they recommend.**

Never underestimate the power of a community raving to the world about your products and services. More people talking about your business translates to more momentum for growth. Apply the five types of social proof in your community, and you'll notice that 1 out of every 5 people you ask to do business with you will either become a customer or a brand advocate and promote your business to others.

Communities get new people excited about your business in a shorter period of time and keep people excited about your business long after they start doing business with you.

# TYPES OF COMMUNITIES

Platforms that allow you to create more than one community optimize your business. Different types of communities help you better leverage social proof and serve those who show interest in your product or service. A customer group unites those who express an interest in becoming a customer with those who are already customers. A brand advocate group is designed specifically for those who wish to take your product or service to the next level of involvement and those who have already met with success as brand advocates.

## CUSTOMER COMMUNITIES

- **Potential Customers:** Do you know people who express interest in becoming a customer? Why convince them to try your product or service alone when you can have a group of excited customers do the work for you? Social proof from others validates that what you're saying is true.
- **Existing Customers:** If you want to keep customers for a long time, provide exceptional customer service. It's difficult —nearly impossible—to service all of your customers in real time without using social media. People stay customers longer when they are in a group with other people who share the same interests and reasons why they're using your product or service. Building a culture around your business creates a movement. Even if a competitor undercuts your price, your customers stay committed to you because they're part of something bigger than themselves, not just buying a product or service.

## BRAND ADVOCATE COMMUNITIES

- **Potential Brand Advocates**: As in the customer community, why do all the work yourself? A space filled with happy and energetic brand advocates inspires customers to change their lives more quickly and efficiently than what you can accomplish alone. Hearing a buzz about potential success is a strong influence, but witnessing and becoming part of that social proof is stronger.
- **Existing Brand Advocates:** Making sure your brand advocates are supported is crucial to the long-term success of your business. These are the people who will sustain your

business for years to come. Invest time to ensure they have everything they need to catapult their growth.

# COMMUNITY POSTS

Create the right culture by knowing the four types of posts that encourage people to interact inside your community.

## ASK QUESTIONS

Asking questions allows you to keep moving forward as a satisfied customer or brand advocate and encourages others with the same question who might be too shy to ask to also move forward when they see the answer. This is proactive customer service. For the introverted in the group or those who don't yet have a question, question posts offer education. Members see answers to questions they may have sometime in the near future. Instead of getting frustrated, they will already know the answer to the question.

If people aren't asking questions in your community, create a post that asks a question. Try, *One of the most asked questions about our product is . . .*

Gayle was one of the funniest women I've known in business. Everything in Texas truly is bigger. She had big blond hair, tremendous blue eyes, and the grandest drawl wrapped around her words. She also had a husband who had a propensity for extreme tidiness. If Tom didn't know where it went or what it applied to, it was trash. Unfortunately, when Gayle took a chance on a skin care line because all the women in her social circle had tried it with great results, Tom got ahold of the box and threw it out, instructions and all. Gayle knew the difference between masks and toners and creams, but as all women will tell you, the order of things is almost—if not *as* important—as the products themselves. Gayle was embarrassed to call customer service and tell them she didn't know how to use the product.

Instead, Gayle turned to the company's customer community. She confessed that she was confused without instructions. Within thirty minutes, a host of people chimed in with the proper order of skin products, and Gayle had her answer. Not only did she have the answer she sought, but her new friends gave her additional hints and tricks so that she could get a better experience with the product. She threatened to use the green mask on Tom while he slept after the next time he was in one of his cleaning moods. I never heard if Tom fully appreciated the skin-refining benefits of the mask.

When you see others ask a question in the community and you know the answer, don't hesitate to respond. Show others that you are a leader and are excited about the business.

## SHARE TESTIMONIALS

Sharing testimonials motivates others who have yet to see the impact of the product or service or business in their lives. Testimonials show others that the future is bright for them as a customer or brand advocate. They hold you accountable to your new friends and give you a good feeling, knowing that the product or service is making a difference in your life and you're telling the world about it. Testimonials validate that you made the right decision in purchasing this product or service or becoming a brand advocate.

My friend LaKeshia understood the power of testimonials. She often shared selfies she snapped while lathering up her skin with a product that helped her maintain her youthful glow. Her confidence was evident in her sparkling eyes and her smile. LaKeshia's testimonial shared the joy of healthy skin.

When LaKeshia posted her fun photos in the community, comments rolled in. Some people who were on the fence about the product she shared became customers after seeing her testimonial post, and others rooted her on with cheers. And because LaKeshia kept compliance at the forefront of her mind, her posts related to maintaining, regulating, and promoting the product kept her business as healthy as her beauty regimen.

When people share testimonials, congratulate them. Say something exceptional. Remember, you are part of a supportive community.

## SHARE TIPS

Sharing tips helps other members of the group get the most out of the product or service or being a brand advocate. Others share their tips, thus helping you get greater impact out of the product or service or business.

I once knew a woman named Charlotte who had an admiration for lipstick. Likely, she could wear a different shade every day for a year and still not have covered her entire collection. Her talent extended to liners and moisturizers and everything in between to make lips look their best. With regularity, she posted videos that shared tips on the latest color trends, how to get color to last, and variables such as clothing colors versus fixed factors such as skin tone. The complexities that women endure to look their best would astound the males of the species.

Charlotte posted her videos for the benefit of her brand advocates. Her brand advocates, in turn, gleaned information, found inspiration, and posted videos for *their* customers. This elevated Charlotte's profile. The end result was that customers benefitted from using the products successfully, and Charlotte helped other brand advocates in the community to flourish.

When someone shares a tip, be sure to comment and share a tip, as well. New tips or reinforcements of old tips, the impact is the same.

## CUSTOMER AND BRAND ADVOCATE UPDATES

Posting an update on how the product or service or business makes a difference in your life is similar to a testimonial except you're updating based on an experience you just encountered.

Regan was a brand advocate who had mastered the art of updates. One day, she would reach out to five people. The next day? Ten people. Mid-week, she often travelled, so she made it a point to talk to three strangers about her business, two of them online, before she rewarded herself with a relaxing evening in her hotel room. When her week's travel was complete, she upped the ante again by sharing her business with ten new people. But here was the catch: the biggest part of Regan's success was holding herself accountable to her peer brand advocates. She checked in on her brand advocate community daily with updates on who, how many, or where she had business encounters. Her travels provided ample opportunity to incorporate cultures and regional differences and gave her a broader perspective for her business. In turn, this motivated other brand advocates to post updates. Before long, other brand advocates posted updates from their travels and diverse regions.

When someone shares a customer or brand advocate update, comment by adding more value to what that person said. It might be as simple as responding, *I love your update!* or *That sounds like a great update. Here's mine.* Again, it's all about building community.

## FREQUENCY OF POSTS

One day, not too long after I first moved to Arizona, I snagged my reflection in a storefront. A dry-cleaning shop, perhaps. Or likely, my favorite drink stop where it was impossible for healthy and delicious to cohabitate. In my new environment, skin was an accessory. Back in Pennsylvania, I hid my body under layers of flannel and blamed the weather for my layer of fat—a crazy, accepted mental place of cold temperatures and lethargy and excuses. But in the cactus-filled landscape of the scorching sun, my excess weight punched out of every shirt sleeve, every waistband, every place where sweat gathered. I thought my reflection was a stranger on the other side of the window until I realized we shared the same clothes, the same lack of hair, and the same heavy chest—inside and out.

Fear launched me into a healthier lifestyle. I cut out all fast food, moved more, and lost 20 pounds. I felt good, but I was still clinically obese. By the time I moved back to Pennsylvania, the land of inertness, I felt like I had done *enough*. Comparison was a mighty excuse.

One year later, I relocated again to the desert southwest. Arizonans were *still* into skin, and I was *still* lost within mine. This time, I was determined to attack my weight issues with consistency. I began a strict 90-day regimen with specific nutritional requirements under the guidance of a body builder named Brewer. Strict cardio, weightlifting, and attention to the detail of how I fueled my body helped me drop an additional 30 pounds. Brewer provided me the most significant lesson in my body's journey to complete health: consistency. At first, Brewer was my constant. I was paying him, after all—why waste that money if I wasn't going to show up every day? After months and a little male bonding, I didn't want to disappoint him. By the time Brewer was no longer a necessity to health, I owned the consistency.

I am your Brewer.

Life is too short *not* to elevate yourself—your dreams, your goals. High-caliber coaching is essential to becoming world-class at anything you attempt. Someday, you may outpace and outperform instruction, but the structure and consistency you put in place now, in your online community, will help it run smoothly.

Brewer is still part of my life. He represents my new consistency, and I refuse to return to the body inside that reflection.

Consistency and frequency go hand in hand.

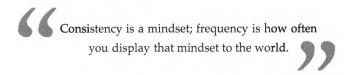

Consistency is a mindset; frequency is how often you display that mindset to the world.

To showcase that communities are active and thriving, frequency plays a vital role. Without frequency, your community looks and feels like a graveyard: silent, quiet, no signs of a pulse. People will wonder if your products or services are really as good as you profess. **If no one is talking about your products or services, how great can the business *really* be?**

## ADMINISTRATOR FREQUENCY

An administrator is someone who creates the community or is added later as a leader after first being a member. Some administrators have full rights to add and remove people, or the group might be structured to give certain administrators limited responsibilities, such as approving posts. No matter how an administrator assumes a leadership position, the community's success is a critical responsibility of the administrator.

As an administrator, post daily. Consistent, fresh content in the group shows new people that the community is flourishing. Robust interaction suggests happiness and has a tremendous impact on people deciding if they want to be a customer or brand advocate. If someone visits on Thursday and the last post was Monday, that person will hear mental crickets. If a product or business is incredible, people should be talking about it frequently. An administrator makes sure this happens by posting daily content that encourages people to respond.

Frequency works. Frequency produces results.

In January 2012, I remember driving the rural backroads near Lancaster, Pennsylvania. Marianne, my future wife, sat beside me. Her parents occupied the backseat. We had spent the weekday browsing the Amish markets—sitting in handcrafted chairs, filling baskets with produce, and eating the most delicious pastries imaginable. It was important to me to make a good impression on my future in-laws.

Mid-afternoon, a call popped up on my cell: a friend I had added to my community, someone I had been waiting to hear from for weeks. He was the leader in a company into which I had stepped to train brand advocates and elevate their social media impact. The last thing I wanted to do was to push aside his call.

Second-to-last thing, actually.

I glanced in the rearview mirror. My future father-in-law's gaze met mine in the reflection. A test? A *what-will-you-do-son* non-verbal challenge? January in the Snow Belt, and I was sweating like we were driving past the equator in goose-down parkas.

By the third ring, I thought I might unzip my skin and crawl out. I had worked all of December to secure a conversation with this guy. I couldn't let it go.

"I'm sorry . . . do you mind if I take this? This guy could really make a big difference in my future." I looked at Marianne. "*Our* future."

Her parents nodded their blessing.

I signaled and pulled into the nearest parking lot. After assuring them I would only be a few minutes, I stepped out of the car and answered the call. For twenty minutes, I paced outside the SUV and put everything I had into the conversation. The connection was fruitful, the call better than I imagined. When I turned my attention back to the car, the windows were fogged from their breathing, like a mini sauna parked near the equator. I climbed back in and apologized. All I could think about was the twenty minutes I had inconvenienced everyone.

Marianne's father reached through the headrest and gripped my shoulder. "You spent the day with us, Jim. We could all spare twenty minutes for your future."

That morning, shortly after waking and coffee, I had set the wheels in motion to support my group, to foster connections, the care and feeding of the relationships that would teach the brand advocates of the company how to thrive in business. After I engaged that morning, I had let the system work its magic, checking in via my cell phone during a few stolen moments during the day. While I sat beside my future father-in-law, trying out handcrafted rocking chairs like two old guys talking about bygone days, the business grew with the frequency that comes with a thriving online community—different people, different schedules, different experiences, at different times. The community grew as life happened. My life.

The leader in this company, my contact, enrolled as a brand advocate. Not because I took the phone call, but because he was impressed with the frequency of action happening in the group. He didn't want to miss out on the group's growth and excitement. How do I know? It was all he talked about on that phone call.

## MEMBER FREQUENCY

A member is someone who joins a community but has no administrative control. While the administrators lead the group, members are the reason for the community's existence. Members add other members, post in the group, and interact with other members' posts, but they serve an even greater purpose. Members engage in spirited discussions, have common interests, and support each other in their endeavors.

If you are passionate about the community's purpose, posting three times a week keeps engagement high. Administrators posting and members liking and commenting on these posts are not enough to sustain enthusiasm. Members must insert fresh content. People need to connect, bond, and build relationships. This happens when everyone is

119

posting and sharing stories. The more posts a new person sees, the more that person will believe in the business and want to experience it, first-hand. This contagious energy is the magic of social proof.

Al had achieved status and fortune in the business world. In his late fifties, he looked back on his career with justifiable pride. At one point, his business was worth a million dollars. He was traditional. Captain of his ship. It took a monumental effort to convince Al to change his perspective when he became a brand advocate.

Leveraging social proof was a foreign concept to him.

Al had always been an expert in his business. The answer guy. He knew his products better than anyone in the industry. On rare occasions when he didn't know something, Al learned that new something backward and forward. So why, when questions surfaced in the community, would he not be the answer guy—quick to knowledge, quick to solution?

Because he is but one person. Sure, Al could bring *everything*. Everything but the extra validation that social proof brings.

One day, I finally convinced Al that his ego, albeit justified, might be best used riding shotgun to the proven process of frequency and social proof. I told Al that his greatest role was as messenger, not the message. **Standing in a crowded room, shouting all the answers through a megaphone is not as effective as the productive hum of an entire room empowered with those same answers.** If Al professed knowledge, it *might* be true. If his entire group conveyed that knowledge with consistency and frequency, it *must* be true. The captain of his ship learned to empower everyone at the helm.

Al was the kind of guy who would have realized a high level of achievement regardless of Predictive Social Media, but at what cost to his timetable, his personal life, and his daily goals? As a messenger, he worked smarter, not harder, and was able to enjoy identical results to what he would have realized on his own.

## MANAGEMENT

Allow members to add people to the community but with one control measure: as an administrator, you must approve their additions. If you don't allow this freedom, you are solely responsible for the group's growth, which is a tough burden for anyone. Use the power of numbers. Let everyone grow the community, together. As a result, social proof will come faster.

Allow members to post content, but you have to approve the posts. This gives you added protection to stop unsavory posts from going out to the community. Remember, you are ultimately in charge of the content. This is the best way to prevent negative social proof from undermining your business.

Upload a strong cover image that represents the community's purpose. If your group is a customer group, the image should represent your products and services. If your group is a brand advocate group, the cover image should capture, visually, why customers would want to become brand advocates.

Some platforms offer an announcement post that remains at the top of your community. An announcement post is the most important post in your community, and it's always saved at the top for people to see. Your announcement post should contain an image because images are more noticeable than text. Along with the image, invite members to review your message—one that inspires people to become a customer or brand advocate. If the platform offers a way to tag members to the announcement post, do so with new members to ensure they find the post easily. Include links that take these new members to videos and other pieces of information that get them excited about your business. Announcement posts are fast becoming the preferred choice over landing pages and websites for a great first impression.

Many platforms offer notification features to all members. Individuals may choose to be notified when others post in the community. Notification is a smart feature to turn on so your members don't miss important posts.

Understanding community features allows you to use every available option to maximize your business. Retain control of approving members and posts so that no negative people or posts infiltrate the community and create negative social proof. Choosing to receive group notifications ensures that you never miss critical information for your business, and announcement posts are the perfect compromise between evergreen content and flexible messages to keep your business fresh.

# TAGGING FRIENDS IN THE COMMUNITY

Kate never met a stranger. Probably because there were no strangers left in our Florida neighborhood. At least, not to Kate. She wore dresses that mimicked how she moved—flowing and whipping around her like curtains at an open window on a gusty ocean-front day. In social situations, she was the breeze—something everyone wanted to be near. She was refreshing and touched everyone with her generous laughter and stories. Kate was infectious with life, and I felt special that she brought me to her gatherings.

But when evenings grew long, Kate's movements grew tired, like being windburned from an all-day sailing trip. Kate did not purposely forget to introduce me to the people she knew. She was simply overwhelmed by the number of friends she had. The excitement of connection pulled her in. It only took a few beach bonfires to want to sink into the sand and wish for a rogue wave to sweep me away from my awkwardness at not knowing Kate's people. Sure, I forged ahead with self-introductions, but to have Kate introduce me would have set me at ease and made me feel like I belonged.

Online friendships are no different.

## ANNOUNCEMENT POSTS

When you're ready to add a friend into the customer or brand advocate community, tag your friend in the announcement post.

Your friends are deciding if they want to be a customer or brand advocate with your business. Make it easy for them to make this decision. The easiest way is to show them where to find the information so they can make an educated decision. All of your best information should be placed in the announcement post. This includes videos, pictures, text, and links to more information. When you tag friends to the announcement post, the platform usually sends them a notification, which allows them to access the desired post effortlessly.

Issac was a faithful man. His spiritual relationship, his love of family, and his impeccable dress were rivaled only by his sentiment toward me. Issac never failed to address me as "Mr. Jim Lupkin."

"Why do you call me so formal like that?" I asked him once.

"Because that's who you are. Mr. Jim Lupkin."

This was Issac's endearment of respect, as much a part of him as his studious eyeglasses and bowtie. The guy had style in spades. I always remember Issac when it comes to this part of teaching him the system because, for all that Issac internalized from my system, every meticulous detail to which he attended, he never tagged friends in the announcement post.

One day, not too long into the system, he grew frustrated. "No one is buying my product."

"You're not tagging friends in your announcement posts. It's important, Issac. It's like leading someone far into a forest and assuming they'll know how to get back to your car because they've seen a hundred trees like the ones you led them past. They don't know where to go, and you're making them do all the work. Worse yet, if they never find their way out of that forest, you might assume they didn't want a ride with you. They'll end up coming out in a different place and finding a ride with someone else."

To his gentlemanly sensibilities, Issac couldn't imagine such a lapse in manners. He began tagging friends and brought his brand of special to a vigorous group.

## INTRODUCTIONS

After you tag your friend in the announcement post, introduce your friend to the rest of the group. You want your friend to meet others and experience the power of social proof. If you do not introduce your friend to the community, other members have no idea that they should be connecting with your friend.

Janet and Shannon had been friends since high school. College took them to different states; marriage took them down different paths of life. Janet became a mom to a big family. Shannon became an attorney. Janet worried for Shannon because, as decades passed, the struggles Shannon had always had with her weight intensified. Janet was into nutrition and had a business selling health supplements where the emphasis was feeling great. Losing weight happened to be a byproduct of taking care of the body. When Shannon confessed that she was tired of living an unhealthy lifestyle but was puzzled and didn't know where to start, Janet took the opportunity to introduce Shannon to her fellow brand advocates by adding her to her customer community.

Immediately Janet's team welcomed Shannon. One man's story, in particular, resonated for Shannon. On the post where Janet introduced Shannon, his welcome comment highlighted his twenty-year struggles with weight—his successes, his failures, his three am binges on his personal kryptonite—nacho chips. This man was all but a stranger to Shannon, yet he had taken the time to write out a heartfelt story and welcome. Shannon wanted to lose fifty pounds; he had lost fifty pounds. In this stranger, who became a friend and, eventually, a fellow brand advocate, Shannon found the courage to take a chance on Janet's product.

Shannon was likely on the fence about trying the product when Janet spoke about how healthy it had kept her all those years and how great she felt while making it part of her overall health plan. Janet had been fairly healthy for the entirety of their friendship, but when added to social proof, the encounter was like mounting evidence in a court case.

Introduce your friend using text, a picture of your friend, or a video of your friend. The most important part of the post is to tell the group members the relationship you have with your friend and why your friend has been added to the community.

Try: *Hey everyone! Please meet Joel. Joel and I have been friends for 9 years. He's a great guy. He asked to be added to this community because he is interested in our product. He's hoping to* (enter reason). *Please welcome him and share your story, especially if you are part of our company for the same reason.*

Talk about your relationship with Joel first because it'll make him feel welcome. He'll know that this is about much more than getting him to do business with you, that there is a real community here of people that know, like, and trust each other. Joel will understand that the group is about friendship first, business second.

The positivity will allow Joel to be receptive to what others say to him in the comments below the post. If you are descriptive on why he wants to be part of the group, members with similar motivation will share personal stories that may help Joel relate. Imagine somebody leaving a comment that says, *Joel, I am just like you.*

This is the power of social proof, done correctly.

## COMMUNITY INTERACTION

Taco festivals are as much a part of living in Arizona as cacti and tumbleweeds. Few outdoor events rival the liveliness and culture surrounding these 100-tent fiestas, complete with native games and a wrestling ring with masked Mexican wrestlers. The object of the festival is simple: stuff your pockets with dollar bills and stuff your belly with as many different one-dollar-tacos as you can eat. A hundred different takes on your favorite food.

As much as I love tacos, I loved the interaction more. The good-natured atmosphere was infectious, the memories spicy. All of it kept me coming back every year.

Now picture the opposite. One hundred white pop-up tents, set apart from each other, with zero mingling. Talk about tumbleweeds. The crunch of hard-shelled tacos would be deafening. Imagine that there was no good-natured smack talk between vendors, no Mexican games played to keep the heritage alive for future generations, no festivalgoers sharing tips on the most unique tacos they had eaten that day.

Interaction is the key to success with festivals, and it's essential for a successful online community. The best of business—the spirited challenges, the sharing of information, the friendly support, the culture of like-minded individuals is found in numbers.

As you visit your customers and brand advocate groups, you'll want to like and comment on other people's posts. A good rule of thumb is to comment when you have something distinctive to say and like or use one of the other emotions, like love, when you enjoyed the post but you're not sure what to say about it.

## COMMUNITY RULES CRITICAL TO SUCCESS

I am a rule-follower. I attack challenges with an instruction manual in one hand and a neatly assembled arsenal of tools in the other. My father-in-law? He doesn't have the patience for step-by-step. Scandinavian, diagrammed instructions from a certain international furniture manufacturer have been known to quicken his pulse and lead to cold sweats. Never was this contrast more apparent than when we got together on a Saturday to assemble a twelve-volt, battery-powered mini-Jeep for my son.

My father-in-law convinced me that he had practically re-built a Ford Mustang in high school. He said *practically* because he had assisted a friend who had more car knowledge. He assured me he was a frequent witness to his friend's automotive talent. Besides, how hard could a toy car be to assemble?

Imagine our pride when we stood back at the project's conclusion to take in the fruits of our manly, not-so-mini labor. Next, imagine that same quickened pulse and cold sweat when my father-in-law realized that functioning parts meant to keep the Jeep running and safe for his grandchild still littered the ground at his feet. Sure, my rule-following method would have added a bit of assembly time, but the end result would have a fully functional mini-Jeep.

If you're like my father-in-law and the thought of sifting through processes and adhering to rules quickens your pulse and breaks you out into cold sweats, I offer a compromise: three rules. Everyone can do three. If you follow these three rules to making a community successful, you'll end up with an end result that doesn't leave forgotten pieces littering the ground at your feet and awkward moments of silence over holiday meals for years to come.

### *Rule 1: Be honest but positive. Social proof can destroy.*

I promise, a day will come when you will grow frustrated about business. No one is immune. Your community is not the place to vent. It's easy for posts to be misinterpreted, to sound like you are complaining about the product or opportunity when, in fact, you are simply looking for answers.

After *every* post you draft, take a breath, fill your coffee cup, stretch your legs, come back to the screen, and then read the post aloud. Ask yourself, *Does this post sound like I'm complaining?* How can I edit the post to retain honesty but stay positive? How can I edit the post to be perceived as someone seeking answers?

---

Honest and **negative**: I bought this product a few months ago, and it's not working. I'm frustrated.

Honest and **positive**: I bought this product a few months ago, and I'm not yet seeing results. I know it works. Can someone help me figure out what I am doing wrong?

Honest and **negative**: I became a brand advocate for this business a year ago, and I still am not making money. Everyone tells me no. I wish the company had better tools.

Honest and **positive**: I became a brand advocate for this business a year ago, and I still am not making money. Everyone tells me no. I know this works. Can someone help me figure out what I am doing wrong?

---

Subtle changes, to be sure. I'm asking you to own responsibility for your success as a customer or brand advocate. Full responsibility makes it easy to be honest and positive instead of honest and negative. Why? Because most people do not want to talk negatively about themselves. They want to find a solution and keep moving forward.

If you're honest and positive inside the community, you create positive social proof while learning and growing. Negativity breeds detrimental social proof.

Before I enrolled in college, I went through a one-year period in my life I'd rather forget. I was in a dying town with no opportunities, earning seven dollars an hour by driving greasy auto parts from shop to shop. The truck stunk. My clothes and hands stunk. My life stunk. I was in a dark place, unable and unwilling to express myself effectively and picking frequent arguments with family and friends.

At the end of that year, my first daughter was born. As kids tend to do, she shifted the axis of my world. I wanted her to be proud of her dad. I wanted to give her a life more ambitious than smelly trucks and smelly hands. I enrolled in college and pulled myself out of my mindset that, frankly, stunk.

College was filled with driven people. They expressed themselves in ways in which I struggled, often far more eloquently, but with one game-changing difference: they offered solutions. And that positivity, that quest to do better, to be better, to seek out and offer better answers, was magnetic. Simply being in the company of these hungry, positive entrepreneurs was enough to make me believe that the vision I had for my baby daughter was possible.

**Be that light for your community. Settle for nothing less than constructive honesty.** Stay on the positive side of social proof.

### *Rule 2:* No luring customers as a brand advocate

When you're a brand advocate, the power of community is heady. Intoxicating. The dynamic of people working together to create something larger than themselves is a self-affirming high, no matter the objective.

Independent contractors and influencers keep the power locked away inside them. Someone with a large following on a social media site must be dynamic and engaging and *on* all the time or his followers slip away. If an independent contractor or influencer posts about a product that helped her lose weight, the product's company is likely to see a bump in sales. Independent contractors and influencers feed the beast of what their followers want in order to retain them. Not everyone has the personality, the dedication, the endurance to sustain influencer status alone.

Brand advocates unleash the power of community. Instead of one influencer being the lynchpin to success, power is distributed among all influencers, resulting in greater influence for everyone involved. Because of this factor, trust must be high. Everyone in the group *must* support each other. A community will fail if members look out for their self-interests.

In your communities, you will have people who are already customers or brand advocates and those who are thinking about becoming customers or brand advocates. Brand advocates who befriend potential customers added to the community by other brand advocates and lure them into becoming their customers create a sticky dynamic. This happens when self-interests outpace dedication to community.

In this breath, decide the kind of community member you will be. Will you take the high road and preserve relationships between members? Will you be the brand advocate who lifts everyone?

Truth *always* comes out. If you choose to lure other brand advocates' customers, you may lose your position as an advocate with your company or be black balled with the other brand advocates. No one wants to work with people who are only out for themselves. Social media sites are filled with billions of people, so there is no need to engage in behavior that doesn't elevate the entire community. Be the individual that lifts up your colleagues, not a divisive agent acting in self-interest.

### *Rule 3*: Post in the community based on the group topic, not your personal life.

Your personal profile is the place to post about your personal life. Being a member in a community is about discussing topics that relate to the purpose of that community. Your laser-like focus in posts helps to keep a spotlight on the product or service, which, in turn, benefits all and brings out your best *you*.

For example, if you are in a customer community, be the best *you* when it comes to the product. Are you maximizing the product? Do you understand the product? Is your belief in the product high? Having conversations focused on the product reinforces your belief in the product, addresses any questions or concerns about the product, and helps you to get the optimum benefit from the product, thus delivering the product's value to you.

If you are in a brand advocate community, your aim is to be a successful brand advocate. Every one of your posts to the community should focus on business.

Let's say your community centers around championing a health product. Sage River (because that sounds like a surfer dude name) is new to your group. He likes the product, but he's obsessed with catching the next wave. He posts pictures his buddy took of him inside the curl. Others ask him what it's like to be caught inside such a phenomenon of nature. Because surf talk ignites Sage more than his new business, his posts veer off-topic, again and again. Pretty soon, no one in the community is discussing the product and everyone is sharing surfing tales. What happens when a potential new customer joins the group to learn more about the product and finds nothing but photos of longboards and whitecaps? That potential customer will question the product's merit and its ability to engage and change lives if others are so easily swayed away from focused discussion.

Keep community posts focused. Strive for topics that relate to your product or service. Celebrate new people and fresh conversation when others join or ask questions.

# PREDICTIVE CHECKLIST: COMMUNITY

❒ From time to time, remind your community of their freedom to voice concerns about your product.

❒ Seek out expert, celebrity, user, wisdom of the crowd, and wisdom of friends social proof.

❒ Make community expectations clear when members opt in and hold members accountable for actions that do not support that mission.

❒ Asking questions inside the community is proactive customer service.

❒ Sharing testimonials motivates others who have yet to see the impact of the product or service in their lives.

❒ Posting tips helps others get the most out of the product or service or being a brand advocate.

❒ As an administrator, post daily. Consistent, fresh content in the group shows new people that the community is flourishing.

❒ Community members who post three times per week keep engagement high.

❒ Allow members to add people to the community, but you must approve their additions.

❒ After you tag your friend in the announcement post, introduce your friend to the rest of the community.

❒ Do not vent inside your community. Stay positive.

*Looking ahead:* Back in 1995, I was a mess. An eighteen-year-old kid in small town, Pennsylvania, trying to figure out the world of business. Every other way to acquire customers in those days failed me. I dropped business cards in restaurant fishbowls and cold-called people out of the yellow pages because I was eating jellybeans for dinner and the old guard told me that was the right way. Everything I didn't know about sales and marketing felt like a heavy raincoat on my shoulders.

Stumbling across AOL and Yahoo Chat gave me the same low-cost connection opportunity, but it actually worked. People listened to what I had to say. I made friends first, did business second. I learned that genuinely caring about people and being passionate about my product was enough.

The same applies here. Social media is low-cost and relationship-first. No formal sales and marketing degree needed. Once you understand how to talk to people the right way, you simply need to know how to talk the right way *to more people*. In the next chapter, we'll explore the numbers. At the intersection of relationships and numbers, Predictive Social Media excels.

# CHAPTER NINE

## Connection

ONCE UPON A TIME, a writer wove stories of faraway places and love and the manipulation of time. She happily existed in her land of fiction, writing and editing and coaching others who crafted their stories, until a day came when one of her clients also happened to be a great businessman.

During the writing of a previous book, I showcased a business acquaintance who had tremendous success in his direct sales business. He was an inspiration I wanted to share with my readers.

You guessed it: her business guy and my business guy were one in the same.

I needed an editor. In a pinch, she stepped in and edited my book, while protesting that business writing was not her lane. She loves to say, "Everyone has a story to tell." I told her businesspeople were no different.

To my writing, she brings heart and, sometimes, a touch of those faraway places and the whole never-enough-time thing. Laura, who writes and freelances under the pseudonym L.A. Mitchell, and I have been working together for six years, through countless projects, high highs, and low lows. Our connection may have started through a mutual acquaintance, but we continued as friends. Her network in the publishing world is now intertwined with my network in social media. Great things are in the works for the union of these two worlds.

You never know when a connection will grow into something magical. The idea of connecting with others gets many people excited because, by nature, people are social. People want to be connected.

One common frustration entrepreneurs and business owners share is running out of people to talk to about their products and services. Maybe you already spoke to everyone you know. Worse yet, you don't know anyone who is looking for your product or service.

Accessing an endless supply of potential customers and brand advocates while building real relationships with real people happens using Predictive Social Media. Based on one social media site's current user base, if you contacted thirty people every day for your business, it would take you 164,384 years to contact everyone the right way. When I say you'll never run out of people to talk to, I mean it.

# NUMBERS

Ever take a close look at the numbers on your house keys? Much of our daily lives revolve around all manner of locking and unlocking and securing and opening, yet we never pay attention to the imprinted numbers on the keys.

With the key numbers and a manufacturer's stamp, any locksmith can reproduce a key to fit inside a lock. They can produce a lock in which that key will work, all without having ever laid hands on the original key. Nineteenth century technology that rules much of our modern world, impossible without numbers.

I went to college for Entrepreneurship and Finance in my early 20s, where I learned the sage advice that to be successful in any business, you need to know your numbers. Production costs, expenses incurred to sell the product, price points, and so much more comprise these all-important figures. Without understanding numbers, how does a business know if it is performing well or failing?

Connecting with others using my system is no different.

For a year, I coached a haircare company on how to use Predictive Social Media. The company loved sending samples to potential customers. The company's owner, Steve, was the quintessential salesman—division Z basketball coach physique, hair slicked back, an abundance of words with not much to say.

In one training session, I asked, "How many samples do you have to send in order to create one new customer?"

I might have heard a pin drop. No one knew.

After a few moments, Steve said, "Well, we don't know. Everyone loves our products, so the numbers must be great."

I asked, "What would you consider great?"

Steve shrugged. "Probably one out of twenty-five."

I said, "So you're saying if we get one out of twenty-five people to become a customer after sampling your product using Predictive Social Media, you're going to be happy?"

Steve's face lit up like a scoreboard. "Definitely! Those are great numbers."

Oh boy. This company had no idea what was great or not great. They didn't know their numbers. The company was doing millions of dollars a year in sales only because the product was remarkable for hair. The company was failing its way to success. Imagine what their sales might have been in those early years had they understood the numbers.

I finished by saying, "I'll get you one out of five."

And yes, I helped this company acquire 1 out of 5 people as a customer.

If you send samples as part of your process of acquiring new customers, numbers are as important as when in the process you send samples. The cost savings of not having to send out ten extra samples to get the same number of new customers makes getting the best conversion ratio a worthwhile endeavor.

**New connections lead to new business, so consistently making new friends is one of the keys to your success. Not understanding the numbers aspect of making new connections using social media stifles growth.**

As much as this system works for large companies, like Steve's haircare, with marketing teams and resources, the numbers make even more sense for independent contractors, brand advocates, and small business owners. In these categories of business, nearly every task falls on your shoulders. Do you have twenty minutes in your day to contact ten new people on social media? Sure. Think long term. In thirty days, you will connect with three hundred people. In six months, it grows to 1,800 people. Over a year, you will connect with 3,600 new people. Based on my proven 1 out of 5 numbers, this equates to 60 new customers monthly and 720 customers after one year. What other marketing strategy helps you connect to this many people, build trusted relationships, and retain them as loyal customers, all without spending large amounts of money?

## MODERN MEASURABILITY AND WORD OF MOUTH

Scaling word of mouth is typically the primary concern people have with my system. Business folks are taught that word of mouth is great, but it's not a plan for long-term growth because it cannot be measured. Before the internet, before social media became so intertwined with our daily activities, these folks would have been correct.

Now, you have your pick of social media platforms, with new and exciting sites coming online all the time. The numbers are there. Nearly everyone in the world is there, waiting for you to connect the right way.

**Predictive Social Media captures the magic of word of mouth—the art of relationships—and unites it with a formula to yield measurable and profitable results.**

Word of mouth *does* scale.

The Connection part of my system is how.

## OPTIMIZING LOCAL TO PROMOTE GLOBAL

Connection puts you in touch with everyone in the world who is on social media. Using Connection at the local level, however, builds the strongest relationships because you spend face-to-face time with people. At first, it may sound counterintuitive. How can local relationships take your product or service around the world the fastest?

Perhaps it is in how we define *local*.

Yes, local can be geographical. But it also means local to your soul —what makes you tick.

Local is not just your hometown or current city—where you grew up or where you live now—but any place you land where there's an opportunity to build relationships with people, face to face. Increasingly, local relationships thrive on social media with features like video chat, where everyone in the world *feels* local.

It's no surprise people feel more connected after spending time together. **People are social creatures. They want to be connected. Since connection is vital to our human experience, it makes sense to do business in environments where we have opportunities to meet others face to face.**

## CLOSE FRIENDS

The first tier of Connection is close friends because you spend the most time with these people. If you live in your hometown, you may have grown up with these friends. Maybe you went to the same school and hung out together on weekends. Maybe you don't live in your hometown anymore; you moved away. Close friends in these new areas might be coworkers, friends of your spouse, or people with whom you share a common interest, like martial arts or cooking. In all instances, these friends are part of your inner circle. They are your go-to connections for quality time.

You might find these people quickly wanting to be a customer or a brand advocate because of the relationship you've built together over time. Nine years ago, I lived in Scottsdale, Arizona. Alexanne and I became close friends. Not a weekend went by that we didn't hang out. We celebrated many holidays and special occasions together. Alexanne is the kind of person you'd want beside you if your business was on the line and a Fortune 500 CEO gave you an ultimatum: impress me or you're history. She's articulate and structured and poised when she needs to be and completely down to earth and fun all the other times. I only know these details because she is a close friend. She's always open to what I have to share with her. Today, you'll find Alexanne and me talking about hot topics through social media despite living more than 2,000 miles apart.

## ACQUAINTANCES

The second tier of Connection is acquaintances. You hang out with these friends from time to time; however, you're really building your relationship through social media by liking and commenting on each other's posts. Like the first group, they may live in your hometown, but perhaps you were never really close. You found these people on social media and wanted to stay in touch. Every now and then, you see someone out and about. You strike up a conversation then it moves back to staying in touch online. Perhaps you live in a new area and have hung out with someone a few times. You like hanging out with this person, but you don't have much in common. When something arises of common interest, like a mutual love for fishing, you call this person to join you. You continue your relationship on social media until the next common-interest occasion arises.

Rosemary and I have an age difference of twenty-eight years. Our definition of fun differs, but we share a common interest. Rosemary and I both want to teach entrepreneurs how to connect with their dreams. Rosemary is a forty-year veteran in small business.

Over the years, we spent time together and kept in touch through social media. When something arises that has to do with entrepreneurship, Rosemary or I reach out to each other. Sometimes it's to update each other with current trends; other times we chat to share new opportunities. Rosemary is one classy lady. She dresses to impress and uses eloquent words to express herself—especially when talking about her passion for collecting antique cars. How do I know this? Because when we connect about entrepreneurship, we always take a moment to learn something about each other. It's important to us that our friendship expands beyond the commonality that brings us together.

## PEOPLE YOU DON'T YET KNOW

The third tier of Connection is comprised of people you don't know . . . *yet*. You'll meet these people when you are out and about, through random chance or through social media. Social media is fast becoming the new local.

This was never more evident than in the way the world stayed connected during the global coronavirus pandemic in 2020. By necessity, video became the face-to-face norm and opened up the entire world to a conversation. Video chats take less time and money spent driving around town and are an efficient way to connect with more people from anywhere in the world. As time and technology advances and everyone becomes more comfortable with video, growing relationships through video chat will become easier. Video features on platforms make it easy to move someone from third to second to first tier as quickly as traditional face to face.

About seven years ago, I traveled to St. Louis, Missouri. While at the airport, I met a bubbly woman named Lisa with an infectious smile. Her massive backpack suggested a Himalayan trek, but its familiar logo told me that we had the same event destination. We also realized we were both from Phoenix. We exchanged contact information and stayed in touch on social media.

Over the years, we have built a cool relationship. Because of our geographical distance, I've only had a few face-to-face experiences with her. However, social media has become the new local for us. Through social media, I learned Lisa is an avid hiker—thus, the backpack—and volunteers her time to non-profit organizations that make people's lives better. Being supportive is second nature to Lisa. She has learned a lot about me as well. We have developed a wonderful friendship through social media.

What do Alexanne, Rosemary, and Lisa mean to your business? Because of the relationships I built at the local level with each of these outstanding individuals, I have real relationships with real people on social media. Some of these people will do business with me because they know, like, and trust me. You have the same type of people in your life and will meet more who fit the criteria.

## HOW WORD OF MOUTH SCALES

The growth of your business accelerates as you apply the Predictive Social Media system. The following is an example of how word of mouth scales on social media.

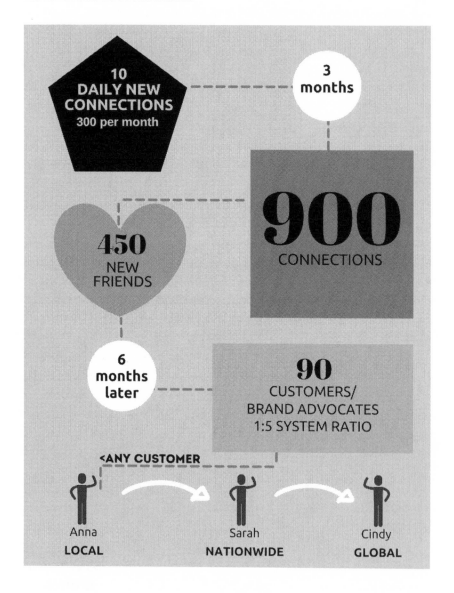

You meet 10 new people every day within a few hours' drive of your business on social media using Connection (how I met Alexanne, Rosemary, and Lisa).

After three months, you've connected with 900 new people; about half, or 450 new people, when using the system the right way, will accept your friend request and stay connected with you on social media.

Six months later, 90 of those 450 decide to become your customer. (1:5 ratio of the system)

Anna, one of your 90 customers, is ecstatic with the results of your product. She shares the product with Sarah, her cousin, on the other side of the country through social media. Anna is now a brand advocate for your company.

Sarah becomes a loyal customer and refers others because of the product benefits.

Sarah tells Cindy, her best friend, about the product one day while chatting on social media. Cindy tries the product and also falls in love with the results. Cindy lives in another country.

Congratulations! You're now global.

This example happens over the course of 12 months with only 1 of your 90 customers. What if this scenario happened with 20 of your 90 customers or all 90? Exciting!

Think about it. Would you pick up the phone and call your friend about a product or service? Probably not. More likely, you'd post a picture of the product or service on your favorite social media site because you love it so much and it only takes ten seconds. Now all of your friends are exposed to it. People love talking to their friends and family about things they like. Social media makes it easy.

## A REMINDER

Before we get into numbers and outreach, I want to drive home my earlier point about cherishing relationships above business.

Another friendship I lost early in my entrepreneurial ventures was David. For him, the business was about personal development. He was shy and awkward around strangers. At one event, he knelt to the ground and pitched long-distance phone service to a girl no older than ten because he was too shy to pitch to adults. Though we were peers, equal members on the same team, the higher-ups in the company often invited me to speak on stage at events. Important people noticed me for things beyond the thrift store clothes and government assistance of my past.

My ego swelled.

While traveling with David and two other team members to an event in Baltimore, I took a phone call in the airport shuttle that ran long. The van stopped in front of our hotel. I glanced at David and said, "Hey, grab my bags and bring them to my room." I finished my call poolside.

After, in the hallway outside our rooms, David's shyness was no longer present. He paced the geometric patterns in the carpet. His voice overpowered the drone of housekeeping's vacuum a few doors down.

"I'm here because I believe in you," David said, "but you can't treat me like this."

I glanced at the suitcase he'd placed outside my door. At that moment, getting sucked up in the vacuum rollers would have been preferable to facing the inconsiderate person I had become. My behavior was unacceptable. Worse, I had ordered him around in front of a group of our peers. I went to Baltimore believing David could learn a few things from me, but David taught me the greater lesson. Although I apologized many times, David and I grew apart because he no longer believed I valued our friendship over business.

Shortly after my experience with David, I started reading personal development books. One of the first books I read was *How to Win Friends and Influence People*. The author, Dale Carnegie, is quoted as saying, "You can make more friends in two months by becoming interested in other people than you can in two years by trying to get other people interested in you."

Truer words have never been spoken.

Remember David. Remember my nursing home hallway encounter. Elevate those around you. Assert kindness into your online spaces and require the same of others. Be that light and your business will follow.

## DAILY ACTIVITY

Contact 10 new people per day as your baseline.

Are you feeling a little more ambitious? Contact 20 new people per day.

For those looking to build the biggest businesses in the shortest amount of time, contact 30 new people per day—10 people in the morning, another 10 in the afternoon, and your final 10 in the evening.

Going above 30 people per day is not recommended because your intent is to build real relationships, not just build business. If you connect with too many people too fast, it will be difficult to build real relationships with everyone. Also, if you contact more than 10 people at one time, you may tend to write the same message. Similar messages come off as spam on social media. Ever get a warning while sending messages that forced you to pick out images in a box? Most likely, it's because you're contacting more than 10 people at a time.

As you become comfortable with Connection, you'll find it only takes one minute to contact a new person. In truth, it may take longer because you enjoy learning more about the person before sending a friend request. This is a great sign that you're putting friendships above business.

## NEVER RUN OUT OF PEOPLE TO TALK TO

The social butterflies among you will have no problem reaching out to 10, 20, or 30 people per day. For those who find Connection more challenging (and for the butterflies), here are some great sources of potential friends. Remember, most people in most areas around the world who have access to the internet are active on a social media platform. Connect with them through social media in the following ways.

## GRADE SCHOOL THROUGH HIGH SCHOOL

A couple of years ago, I reconnected with an old friend named Raymond on social media. The most persistent memory I have of Raymond is traveling beside him on a school bus to a mining camp field trip in fourth grade. We played a travel game of magnetic checkers and hung out together all day. Raymond and I had known each other since kindergarten, but our interests diverged about halfway through our school career. He was gifted with taking cars apart and putting them back together, and I gravitated more toward the baggy-pants, hip-hop crowd. I hadn't spoken with him since eighth grade.

After a few months of staying in touch on social media, Raymond sent me a message: *Hey Jim . . . I noticed you are doing well as an entrepreneur, and it looks like you're doing something with building businesses on social media. At work, I had some friends introduce me to a business opportunity. I'm not sure if these opportunities are any good. My wife and I would really love to make some extra money. Can you help?*

Think about the significance of this message. Raymond and I hadn't spoken in twenty-four years. We had engaged on each other's posts weekly for a few months. He has friends at work, likely going years back, yet he asked me for advice. Why? It's about trusted relationships and inspiring others with what you do. On a memorable field trip, somewhere between mining camp tours and checkers, we forged a bond. Time passed, but the trust never disappeared.

School connections are the first place to start when growing your list on social media. You'll be exposed to thousands of new people from school connections because you probably knew each other—or at least knew of each other—and grew up in the same area.

You might be thinking that you graduated too long ago or that you didn't have many school friends. Maybe you didn't graduate at all. These common concerns disappear quickly as you start to reconnect and realize some people have changed and some have not. Others, you'll be surprised to learn, are just like you.

If your chosen platform allows you to sort users by school or graduating class, do a search for those peers. Hashtags related to reunions might work, as well. If your platform doesn't have this feature, pull out your old yearbook (less than ideal because it doesn't account for married name changes) or look up your classmates on one of the free online sites and download a list.

Next, connect with people from other years. I graduated in 1996, so I'd want to connect with people who graduated during all three years before me because I was a freshman, sophomore, and junior when these people were seniors. I'd also want to connect with those who graduated during all three years after my graduating year because these people were freshman, sophomores, and juniors when I was a senior. We probably all know each other, recognize each other, or have mutual friends on social media. The common ties of going to the same school makes the trusted relationship happen faster than meeting a stranger.

It's always wonderful to watch people's expressions light up when they reconnect with forgotten friends. Life may have pulled them in different directions, but social media is a great unifier.

## COLLEGES AND UNIVERSITIES

Not long ago, I reconnected with a college roommate, Ryan. He was a talented chef, a lady's man, and never seemed to have a dull day. Ryan was one of those cool guys on campus. As with most college friends, careers got in the way and we drifted apart. Since reconnecting on social media, we've stayed in touch.

After six months of developing the relationship on social media, Ryan sent me a message: *What's up? I know I teased you about all those business deals you had going in college but look at you now. From what I see you posting on social media, you're killing it. I always knew you'd do something with all those crazy entrepreneurial ideas. I'm looking to do something new. Can you help me or put me in touch with someone?*

As with school, trusted relationships take root in college. Ryan and I stayed in touch the right way on social media, which eventually led to me helping him. I referred him to the right people, and he is now following his passion.

With college connections, you have the potential to be exposed to tens of thousands of people because of the size of many colleges.

Do you want to connect with others who have similar life experiences as you? Absolutely. Having common interests and experiences makes real connections happen quickly. College is a great commonality to leverage, as long as it's done correctly.

The difference between a grade school and college social media search is that you may not want to reach out to everyone who graduated in the same year due to class size. In this case, choose people you remember and those who share mutual friends. As in your school search, connect with everyone who graduated three years before and three years after your graduation year.

Once, I challenged myself to see how far back in time I could go and still create a relationship. I found a guy who graduated from my college in 1975. I attended college from 1999-2002. I sent Charles a message: *Hey Charles! Looks like we both went to Johnson & Wales University. Only difference is you graduated in 1975, and I went to school from 1999-2002. Hope to connect.*

A couple of weeks after I sent this message, Charles responded with intrigue. We talked about how much the campus had changed and what new majors were available. I'm still friends with Charles today. If you are passionate about your college's sports teams, you can bet other alumni are too. Alma matters create robust affinities.

Attending the same college builds trusted relationships. Something worth pursuing.

## HOMETOWN

My friend's father, John, was a stylish businessman in my hometown. He sported three-piece suits from the big city, a fat gold watch, and shiny loafers with fancy stitching. I have no idea what he sold, but it wasn't door-to-door encyclopedias. As a young and inexperienced entrepreneur, I wanted a sliver of his success.

The day I pitched John long-distance phone service, I pulled my 1982 Nissan Maxima into his circular driveway and killed the loud engine. Next to the lion sculptures framing the front steps and the groomed rose bushes, I felt like a cheap flier stuck in the door seam—all but the black, faux-leather briefcase I had scraped together enough money to buy. The contents were of little consequence—pens, letters of authorization for my service, marketing brochures, a calculator because it seemed entrepreneurial. The case shined.

I dried my palms on my wrinkled khakis and rang the doorbell. Chimes bounded through the house beyond the glass door. More than once, I considered bolting. The man could afford a long-distance plan to the South Pole. What could he possibly want from an eighteen-year-old kid?

John answered the door in a polo shirt and golf pants. He smiled like he was on vacation, shook my hand the way he must have a million transactions in some high-rise in Philly—all let's-play-18-holes grip and a pump of reassurance.

The first ten minutes of my pitch, I could have floated the dining room table in sweat. My words poured out like a used car salesman.

"Take your time, son," John said. "You're doing great. I like what I'm hearing."

I felt like I had surfaced after a near-drowning presentation.

From then on, I took my time, stopped raking my hand through my then-hair, and chronicled examples of the remarkable savings my service brought past customers. Turns out, John didn't want to spend his hard-earned money to call the South Pole. Saving 40 bucks on long distance meant another round of golf. And golfers have many friends. Within six months, John had referred hundreds of customers to my service. John became my first lesson in hometown connections.

Hometown connections expose you to hundreds of thousands of people, depending on where you live. My hometown has a population of 19,000. When you add in the nearby towns (all the areas seem to be connected in one way or another), the population numbers increase to 60,000. An hour away from my hometown is a city with a population of 250,000.

These people all have the same roots as you. The deeper the connection, the more profound the relationship. The best relationships do business together in the biggest ways. Use hometown advantage to make new connections and grow your business.

Remember not to prejudge. John lived in a town of 60 people, yet he worked in my hometown and knew most of the business owners.

My friend Martha grew up in a town of 700 people. She was hesitant to contact people in her hometown because she lacked confidence that people from so far back in her past would want to connect with her. She wanted to focus on her current town because the population was 5,000.

I said, "Just give it a try. Look at it this way–there are only seven hundred people. You'll contact these people in no time and use it as experience before you start contacting everyone in your current town of five thousand."

Within a few weeks, Martha's feedback was impressive. She told me story after story of how she connected to hometown people. Not only did she reconnect with many friends, her business grew to nearby towns that had populations in the hundreds of thousands. Her confidence grew exponentially. All of this happened from a town of only 700 people.

## CURRENT CITY

Erin and I met at a coffee shop because a friend referred her. My friend told me that Erin was someone I needed to know in town. Erin was one of the most networked women in Scottsdale, Arizona. She hailed from Alaska, loved attending events, and knew every reporter and journalist in town.

I presented Erin with my services. She replied, "Give me your service for free, and I'll send you many referrals." I had just started the business and didn't yet have one customer. I had been burned by empty promises before, but Erin was clearly connected. Reluctantly, I agreed. Within a month, Erin had sent me more than a dozen people. Ten became customers.

We both lived in Scottsdale, and I wanted to do business locally. This would've been more of a challenge had we lived in different states. I had the opportunity to spend an hour with Erin, getting to know her and building trust. Had this introduction happened today, I might have reviewed all her social media profiles before meeting her for coffee to make sure we had commonalities.

It's possible to connect with a significant number of people in your current city, depending on the city's population. This group yields grand connections because you are able to combine the power of social media with the ability to meet people in person.

The current city search can overwhelm because some cities have millions of people. Connect with those whom you would want to be friends outside of business. If you can't determine if the connection is ideal by the initial search, click on the person's name and profile.

## INTERESTS

Common interests allow you to connect with people who might already have a curiosity about your product or service. Making connections with those who share common interests result in an endless supply of friends.

This way of finding people connects you with others who already buy products or services similar to yours. If someone is already buying, they might consider buying from you—assuming your offer is comparable in quality and price—because you are trying to establish a relationship.

I once had a dental care business. I never thought I could get excited over toothpaste. However, this toothpaste felt great compared to what I was using at the time and left me with that fresh, clean feeling after brushing. The mouthwash gave a tingling feeling when I gargled. Wonderful products. I contacted Don because we were both entrepreneurs. I thought he would be a good candidate to expand my business into a new area, not just because he was a breathing mammal who brushed his teeth, but because we always talked about working together. I shared the products, and he liked them. I asked Don if he would be interested in expanding these products throughout Florida. He seized the opportunity. In four months, Don and his team of brand advocates produced $100,000 in product sales. That's a lot of tooth-paste and mouthwash.

Focusing on people who already buy similar products evolves into new business. If someone is already buying a similar product or service and you are convinced your product is better quality and price, then that person should be your customer.

## MUTUAL FRIENDS

Rick reached out to me on social media. He was in the beginning stages of learning how the internet worked. He was analytical and detail oriented. At first, growing a business on social media seemed out of his comfort zone, but because he was a man who broke every-thing into a process, I quickly realized he, and others like him, would be successful if I took what I did instinctively with clients and turned it into a system. In the same way Six Sigma had created a consistent and methodical pathway to results, a social media system allowed me to help grow large companies and small businesses all over the world. Following the system was comparable to having me beside them at all hours.

Over the years, the system I shared with Rick evolved and expanded into Predictive Social Media. Rick and I have built a strong relationship. We talk about social media and inspire each other. We are close enough that he confided that my early system felt like training, but this—*this* elevated and predictive system was a supercharged level of social media for business. His passion and the results his business experienced with Predictive Social Media is unmatched, even by the early version of my system.

Rick is a brand advocate for a wellness company. He was so excited about Predictive Social Media that he introduced me to David, a corporate executive with his company.

This introduction is an example of how using mutual friends during the Connection step works. I might have never met David without knowing Rick, without social media having constructed that bridge.

David and I connected and hit it off right away. Our core values aligned on the first call. We worked together for the next twelve months. Nearly every turn, every moment, every action, validated how alike we were—one of those rare business relationships. Since this new connection, working together, our businesses exceled. We have done business in Mexico, the US, Canada, Australia, China, and Taiwan.

One of David's brand advocates for his company acquired 175 customers in 7 months using the system. I received a heartfelt message from her on social media, talking about her success and how her life has forever changed.

I shared her words with David. During an emotional phone conversation, we allowed it to sink in how one connection through a mutual friend, Rick, changed this woman's life so dramatically for her and her family.

Connection is a noteworthy force.

The best part of Connection? David and Rick and I will be lifelong friends, no matter where we go with business.

Be a special part of Connection, as well. I love it when readers, like Rick, reach out to me. I love it when readers connect me with others, like David. Relationships are why I do business.

You may have heard the phrase "six degrees of separation." It's the idea that it takes six or fewer connections (a friend of a friend) to connect with anyone in the world.

**According to research done on social media in 2016, each person in the world (social media users only) is connected to every other person by an average of three and a half other people.**[7] **Social media has redefined the idea of mutual friends by making the world a smaller place.** Mutual friends connect you to everyone on social media.

Mutual friends are the most effective way to make unlimited new connections. Why? Remember, for people to do business with you, you must have a relationship with them.

Instead of starting a new relationship from scratch, piggyback off of the like and trust factors created by your mutual friend. What if your mutual friend knew this person with whom you are connecting for 20 years? That is 20 years of like and trust bonds built. What if it was 3 or 5 years? Still much longer than the time you spent with this mutual friend, which begins at zero.

Like and trust takes time to develop. You cannot speed it up by doing fancy marketing. Instead of starting at zero, mutual friends give you a head start on the relationship. It's a short mental and emotional hop from your friend thinking *if she is friends with this person* . . . to *she must be like my friend.*

**Mutual friends are so influential, you should add them into all of the other ways you use Connection.** For example, if a new connection from your current city has 34 mutual friends, pick a mutual friend, someone with whom you have a real bond, and mention that friend's name in your message to this new connection.

## ONLINE COMMUNITIES

People love to connect with others who share commonalities. Think about your closest friends. What do you have in common? You probably like similar food, sports teams, clothes, or entertainment venues.

Online communities allow connections between large groups of people who have similar interests. Build relationships with people like you, twenty-four hours a day, seven days a week, from your laptop, notepad, or phone.

**The days of being friends with people simply because you live close are over. Connect with people that you love being around because you have the same common interests.**

A friend of mine once invited me to join her online community where people supported each other on all things business-related. I'm always up for encouraging others in business, so I happily accepted. A few months later, I saw a post from a member of this group: *can someone give me advice about how to use social media to grow my business?*

By the time I read the post, it had more than 30 comments. Some answers were well-intentioned but misguided. Some answers were flat-out wrong. A few were frightening. My specialty is helping people use social media effectively for business, so I joined in and wrote a few sentences.

Within days, a few people from the group who had read my comment reached out to me privately to tell me how much my perspective resonated with them. All four were genuine, ambitious business owners who had a fire in their hearts to change their lives and expand their achievements. As a result of that one comment, I made four new friends who were passionate about business.

## EVENTS

I used to be a business event junkie. Connecting with like-minded people at these semi-local events fueled my appetite for networking. Soon, however, the cost of attending so many events added up. While my wallet shrank from the gas and restaurant expenses associated with travel, my waistline expanded from all the time sitting in the car and not being active. In the end, I rarely made more than a few key contacts. Hardly justifiable. I was out a bunch of business cards with no real follow up from myself or the people I met. I needed a better strategy almost as much as I needed a bigger belt.

A winning strategy turned out to be a small investment of time on the front end of each event by using the event feature inside the most popular social media site in the world. Not only did I gather advanced information about events that I wanted to attend, events expanded my awareness of other meetups I didn't know about. In addition, I browsed through the list of those who planned to attend an event, searching for those with whom I had a great deal in common and could build a relationship first, business connection second. I reached out privately to future attendees who fit that criteria. Those who replied became an event priority for me.

Events were now selective and strategic. I no longer wasted time. Now, in a room of 100 people, 10 were already primed to meet in person. The quality of our interaction elevated, as well. Because I had visited these people's social media profiles to become familiar with their likes and interests and had already established a connection via social media, our in-person time strengthened our ties exponentially. After the event, we continued to grow our relationship. Almost always, in time, these relationships evolved into business.

Events are a plentiful resource to build pre-relationships, connect with people face to face, and continue relationships online. Nearly every platform has a way to announce and spread the word about upcoming gatherings of people with similar interests. Find out what's going on in your local area and who is attending these events. Reach out and establish a friendship before the event starts. Then you'll attend the event already knowing people.

One Halloween, I wanted to take my son to do harvest-type activities, like cornfield mazes and painting pumpkins. I logged onto social media to see if there was anything in the area and found three places with some serious fun potential. After checking out some photos from the previous year, I noticed that two of my friends, Mary and Amanda, planned to attend one of the events. I sent Mary and Amanda messages, asking them about their experiences. Although we were already friends on social media, the conversation expanded our relationship.

I then took the Halloween event a step further. I chose three people under the event's section who planned to attend and who seemed to have a great deal in common with me but with whom I was not yet friends. I sent them each a message that said I was thinking of attending the event and asked if they recommended it. Debra was one of the three who responded back. We engaged in a fun conversation. One year later, we are still friends on social media.

In the past, creating an event meant sending out invitations and calling everyone to give details of the event. Now, creating an event on any platform takes only a few minutes—as simple as combining text with enticing images and inviting friends.

Since using events, I've felt more connected to my community than ever before. I know what's going on in town. Events are a perfect way to bring together a local community.

## THE PSYCHOLOGY OF CHOOSING SOCIAL MEDIA FRIENDS

Connection may expose you to everyone, but it doesn't mean you'll become friends with everyone. You're probably somewhat particular who you befriend in person. Apply those same rules to making friends on social media. If not, you will find yourself with thousands of friends you don't really know.

**A key factor in reaching out and building quality relationships is searching for a common denominator.** Think about your personality, your likes, your experiences, your hobbies, and anything else that sparks conversation in you.

Somehow, in my freshman year at college, I was allowed to choose my own classes. This was after the registration office informed incoming students that the school computer system selected classes. I assume I had freedom of choice for one of two reasons: I tried to choose my classes anyway and the computer didn't stop me, or I was a twenty-two-year-old freshman and the registrar felt pity that I had started college four years late (I got sidetracked running my first business). Whatever the reason, I chose a few classes out of order. The results were catastrophic. My class on federal taxes met in a dungeon-like, subterranean classroom with no windows. The class was a circle of Dante's Inferno. Every word out of the professor's mouth, every sentence out of the tome-like textbook, was a foreign language. I was completely lost within a few days because I didn't take my prerequisite classes. The prerequisites would've prepared me for more advanced classes.

I realized the importance of starting right, and I carried this priceless lesson into social media. If you don't start correctly by choosing the right social media friends, then you will not build trusted relationships with people who may do business with you.

You might think that everyone needs your product or service. I used to think the same way.

More than fifteen years ago, I owned a dietary supplement business. My product was needed and wanted by every human being on the planet. After all, the supplement balanced the immune system. If the immune system was overbalanced, it indicated an autoimmune disease. If it was under balanced, sickness was likely. The supplement was backed by science and clinical studies. It worked, and my product would change the world!

My first conversation with a potential customer went something like this: *Hey Arlene! I found the most amazing product, and I want you to take it. It makes your immune system strong. You see, there is this thing about balanced, underbalanced, and overbalanced, etc. You're not going to believe this—the company has science and clinical studies. This means with 100% certainty, you will see results. Can you try it?*

Guess what happened next.

Arlene smiled and responded, *Oh, Jimmy! I'm not drinking that stuff. I feel wonderful. I eat well. I don't get sick much. I'm fine. Why don't you get in touch with Susie?*

Everyone might need your product, but until someone wants the product, it doesn't matter.

Thanks to social media, you connect with people based on many factors. But how do you focus on those who are most likely to become a customer or brand advocate? Remember, you're still using the suggested commonalities, like hometown and online communities, but within those commonalities, the potential number of connections can still overwhelm. So, we narrow the list again.

To answer the all-important question—*with whom should I connect?* —consider the following:

- Since you've been in business, what commonalities do you notice about those who purchase your product or service?
- Are most of your customers female or male? If females favor your business, then focusing on males could hinder growth.

Imagine selling make-up remover to Uncle Teddy who is single, collects arachnids, and works construction. I may have tried that.

- Do most of your customers suggest an age group? If people between the ages of 30-40 years old tend to buy more from you, then speaking with 18-29 years old may slow your growth. Picture yourself trying to sell home electricity service to a 19-year-old who is still in college. I may have tried that also.
- Do most of your customers appear to be married, single, or another status? If those who are single contribute more to your business, then focusing on married couples may stagnate your business. Trying to sell singles meetup event tickets to Bob and Carol, a married couple with two kids, a dog, and a cat, will be a waste of your time. If Bob takes you up on selling singles tickets, he may land a permanent sleeping spot on the couch. Fortunately, for Bob's sake, I never tried that one.
- Do most of your customers live in a particular area? If people lean more towards your business from one region of the country and you're growing your business in a different region, it may take longer to see results.

Reflect on the above questions to understand the perfect customer or brand advocate for your business. Consider factors such as education level, minimum income per year, generation, own or rent a home, work in a specific industry, hold a special job title, and/or have a focused interest. Consider factors unique to your business that may play a role in your connection decisions.

## CHOOSING SOCIAL MEDIA FRIENDS

Thus far, you've determined all the ways to never run out of people to talk to—broad searches such as current city or college. In the last section, we narrowed down these broad friend pools by asking questions related to your product or service sales. Likely, your numbers are still high. Remember, if you can't build a relationship outside of business with these people, they won't do business with you. So, we narrow the high numbers again to ensure you're connecting with people who make building relationships easy.

**Social media connects you to people with whom you would instinctively connect in the real world. This is the primary reason it's possible to build relationships as strong as people build when meeting face to face.** This truth may be the only thing you need to know to relieve the pressure to connect with people you wouldn't consider friends outside of social media.

How can you make better decisions about your social media connections?

Looking at someone's profile photo is an excellent start. Pictures represent people. How do you feel when you first look at someone's picture? Do you smile or frown? If you smile, you want to continue learning more about the person. Frowning isn't bad. It simply means that you don't resonate with this person. Why continue? You won't be successful at building a relationship that could eventually lead to new business if the initial connection isn't there.

I once saw a profile picture of a woman holding a boa constrictor. She had her tongue sticking out, and the expression in her eyes left me unsettled. For some people, this picture would have resonated with their core values and a new friendship would have developed. For others, like me, common ground didn't seem possible. Nightmares, maybe, but no common ground.

Be sure to also browse that individual's posted photos. Pictures influence you towards liking or disliking people because the individual selected the image that best illustrates his or her personality.

I remember a picture of a guy I saw on social media, standing in front of a Ferrari and mansion while showing off his expensive watch and clothes. Attractive women surrounded him. While he may have pulled in new friendships, he also might have turned people away who are not into the materialistic lifestyle.

Next, browse an individual's social media profile. You may learn where this person went to high school or college, her work history, her current city, her hometown, her interests, and more. You'll get excellent insight into the person and quickly determine if building a relationship is possible.

My friend, Tamara, posts the coolest videos of her lip syncing and dancing to hip hop. She creates these videos in her office, at the end of her workday, to relieve stress. When her videos pop up in my newsfeed, I instantly click on them and smile. I love being around happy people, so I love being her friend.

**The surest test for authentic online friends is to ask yourself:** *would I be friends with this person outside of social media?* It's much easier to answer this question when you're clued into the social media images and words people use to represent themselves.

## REACHING OUT FOR THE FIRST TIME

Now that you've narrowed down your search to the best candidates to be real friends with, what do you say when reaching out to them for the first time? For some people, following this outline helps.

1. Why you're reaching out
2. Mutual friend or something in common
3. Call to action

In the examples below, I've separated out two scripts based on either a mutual friend or something in common. Remember, as with all examples, make them unique to you.

**Mutual Friend Example**: *Hi Kelly! I'm reaching out because it looks like we both grew up in the same town. We have 34 mutual friends, and one of them is Thomas Deerheart. How do you know Thomas? I knew Thomas through my cousin, Alicia Gratefell. I met Thomas maybe 5 years ago. Great guy! I'm looking to create more friendships on social media, but only want to connect with people I think I could be real friends with outside of social media. I sent you a friend request. Love to stay connected.*

**Something in Common Example**: *Hi Kelly! I'm reaching out because it looks like we both grew up in the same town. We don't have any mutual friends, but I noticed one of your pictures with your little girls was taken at Rowland Park. I grew up down the street! I'm living out of state, but I know if we were back in town my wife would love to take our kids to that park. Great* *times! I'm looking to create more friendships on social media but only want to connect with people I think my wife and I could be real friends with outside of social media. I sent you a friend request. Love to stay connected.*

## WHEN TO BRING UP BUSINESS TO NEW FRIENDS

**People do business with you when they have a relationship with you, are inspired by you with your business (this happens when they see you on social media talking about your business using the Communication step)** *and* **they have a life experience.** All three factors must be present for someone to engage in a business relationship with you.

Connection is all about that first reach of friendship. Do not bring up business during the Connection step.

On rare occasions, new friends may ask what you do for a living. Tell them about your business but keep the emphasis of those initial encounters to building a friendship. In the next chapter, Communication, you'll learn how to inspire people with your business.

## PREDICTIVE CHECKLIST: CONNECTION

❐ Social media is the new local in a world that continues to shrink.

❐ If you want to build a global business, think local.
Word of mouth scales because social media makes it easy to stay connected to others and share products and services with friends and family.

❐ School, higher education, hometown, current city, common interests, mutual friends, and events are all great ways to make the best connections.

❐ Sending a friend request is not enough. Real success happens when you build relationships. Message your new friend along with the invitation to convey your intent to build a relationship.

❐ Group new connections into friend lists to track your progress and adjust, if needed. Organization is the key to understanding the numbers.

❐ The psychology of choosing social media friends plays an important role in growing your business because it puts you in front of the right people at the right time.

❐ Success begins with understanding demographics, psychographics, and why customers get excited about your product or service.

❐ Features of your chosen platform help you determine the right connections to begin solid relationships. When making new friends, be sure to make the shift in mindset from business-only to friendship-first.

*Looking ahead:* If Connection is the *who* in the social media puzzle, Communication is all about *what, when,* and *how often* to say something. Knowing the right topics to post on social media makes all the difference in growing your business. Many times, I ask my clients, "Do you want to be right or do you want to be successful?" **Communicating the right way is all about casting toxic battle lines aside and filling your social media orbit with messages that lift everyone.**

# CHAPTER TEN

## Communication

GILLIAN ATTENDED one of my 2015 social media workshops in Toronto, Canada. The workshop was put together by Tom, a mutual friend of ours. Later, she wrote about the day, "This event seemed right up my alley. I was in *awe* of the material Jim presented—the system, the process, the analytics, the details. *This* guy had it all figured out. He was doing exactly what I was screaming for my company and all the direct sales companies to do. It was brilliant. I became Jim's biggest fan that day."

For the last six years, Gillian and I stayed in touch on social media. We became friends because we liked and commented on each other's personal posts. We became trusted business colleagues because of the social media mindshare we had through business posts. We discussed new social media sites and updates to existing platforms.

In 2019, Gillian fell ill. Coupled with the loss of her father and father-in-law, whom she cared for at home, grief took Gillian to a dark place where she became progressively worse. By December, poor health forced her to leave her lucrative corporate position. After seven years, recognized as the social media guru of her company, she knew she had to put herself first.

During this difficult time, I checked on her through social media. In addition to walking with a cane, she suffered slurred speech, debilitating headaches, and cognitive delays. Coupled with grief and the loss of her ability to drive, Gillian's challenges mounted. Her traumatic brain injury unraveled her from the strong, independent influencer she had been. She felt trapped inside her body with no purpose; she had to do something significant to change her life's trajectory.

She moved with her family to St. Martin in the Caribbean. The sun and the relaxed tropical lifestyle began to heal her. During this restorative period, I reached out to her, using the methods in the Communication portion of the system. I shared the painful story of losing my mother, and it helped her realize she had not completed the mourning of her mother's passing from cancer.

Loss fed our connection.

When reflecting on how far she's come, Gillian adds, "I have always admired Jim from afar, followed his career, advocated his books and system. Our online check-ins had moved from a like, comment, and share to a heartfelt friendship and increased trust. His check-ins, our conversations, fed the light of hope within me. He got me in touch with my core values. He listened to my voice. He inspired me through his vision to help others. I am fortunate to have Jim as a colleague, a guide, a mentor, a true friend. Today, with the gift of time, healthy living, and a new, heart-centered role working alongside Jim, I can dance, speak, drive, and influence again. I look forward to changing the world with Jim and ending each day with a grin."

Gillian has equally impacted my life. Through my grief, she encouraged me to reclaim my true self. She gave me the courage to pursue a passion that honors my mother. Gillian now plays a significant role in my business. She is relentlessly positive and inspires the team, and me, every day.

The Communication portion of Predictive Social Media is all about developing the new friendships you established in the other Cs. Longevity in your relationships enhances the reach of trust bonds and means you will always have a constant list of people who may look to your business. Longevity, however, takes stamina. Being open to new ideas and perspectives, remaining positive when life gets you down, putting forth the effort when you're tapped out—all of these approaches are essential to prevail.

**For your business to matter to someone, that someone must matter to you—through words and actions.**

# WHAT MATTERS MOST IN COMMUNICATION

Understanding what matters most in building social media friendships will help you optimize success on any platform. Internalize these truths, and you'll be amazed at how your online relationships blossom.

### TIME MATTERS

Stay in touch with people because real relationships take time. People must like you if they're going to do business with you. Some people will genuinely like you within minutes. For most people, that connection takes longer to build.

### LIFE EXPERIENCES MATTER

You don't have to be a salesperson to succeed. People become committed to using your product or service when they have a life experience remarkable enough to internalize the value you offer. Selling to someone without this life experience relating to your product or service is a never-ending cycle. Once you sell, you will always need to sell to that person so that they continue to do business with you. You have conditioned that customer to believe you will do most of the heavy lifting in the relationship. However, if you nurture the relation-ship until someone has a life experience, your business interaction achieves a balance between what you offer and what life is telling your customer he or she needs.

### PAST EXPERIENCES MATTER

How much and how quickly people trust you is largely based on parameters beyond your control. Our past conditions us to hold to beliefs about trust, both positive and negative. Some people grew up in a world where they were protected and supported; therefore, the rate at which they build connection is faster than someone who grew up in an environment where trust was often betrayed. Additionally, their history of dealing with businesspeople in the sales arena may be clouded by those who have not been good stewards of their trust. When building a relationship, understand that you may be inheriting broken trust.

## LONGEVITY MATTERS

**The fastest way to build trust is to stay with your business and not start another one. Longevity in business suggests longevity in relationships.** Stay in touch with friends. Offer updates of the progress you're making in your business. I have been building my social media business for a long time. I never changed course. Trust is high when I talk about this subject.

## SIMPLICITY MATTERS

Speak at an eighth-grade level on social media—most of the time. People like and comment more when you don't whip out silver-dollar words. I used to post with Scrabble-worthy words and ramble on about philosophical topics, but discussing nuclear fusion or the physics of outer space doesn't inspire the same amount of likes and comments as goofing-off photos with my son or family hiking stories. This doesn't mean you dumb down your posts. Be yourself. Be intelligent. But also think of social media as the level of discourse you have when you go to lunch with friends.

## LIKES MATTER

People like posts because they don't have anything meaningful to add to a conversation, but they enjoyed the post enough to share an emotion. Some people have something to say but are shy, don't want to share, or are too busy to take the time. Likes are good. Because your post represents you, likes indicate that people are genuinely starting to like you.

## COMMENTS MATTER

People comment on posts because they have something relevant to say about the content and are willing to spend time to convey their thoughts. Comments are a symbol of trust, from a personal perspective or a business perspective—or both.

## CONTROVERSIAL TOPICS MATTER

**Stay away from controversial topics. Subjects like religion and politics have no place in your business. Do you want your voice to be heard, or do you want to build your business?** In these polarizing times, the two realities are often mutually exclusive. Focus instead on valuing relationships and celebrating comradery between friends. The same applies to liking or commenting on others' controversial posts. Stay neutral, and you'll maintain the like and trust you've worked so hard to build.

Controversial topics can be discussed on social media, but not in the way it's currently being done. Sometimes I touch on controversial topics, but I come at them from a place of wonder, curiosity, a desire to be well-informed, and a way that brings out the best in people.

## EMOTIONS MATTER

Focus on emotions most of the time and facts some of the time. The emotional drive in humans often overpowers common sense. My investment professor in college was fond of saying, "Even the stock market is driven on emotion." **If you touch someone's heart, like and trust will go through the roof.** Sprinkle your interaction with occasional facts, and this heart-first tactic will cement a person's decision to do business with you. I have known this principle for years, and I still struggle to lead interactions with my heart. I am a fact-based, data-driven type of person. My loved ones have done wonders to help me soften those edges and connect with emotion.

## POSITIVITY MATTERS

Most people prefer a positive environment over a negative one. Therefore, if you are a positive person who focuses only on going up, not down, you'll inspire many people to become good friends. **Even in the most negative of situations, positivity can be found.**

In 2017, my mother passed away. The loss had me circling the drain of negativity. I might have derailed everything I had worked so hard to create for me, and for my family, had I not realized how much my mother would have wanted me to find a way to move forward.

What trapped me in my thoughts was the notion that things might have—and should have—turned out differently for her, if only she'd had access to optimal nutrition her small intestines could easily absorb —in the two years leading up to and during her heart crisis—so that surgeons could perform a valve operation. I vowed then and there to use my social media system to change the world of wellness so that others wouldn't experience the pain of deterioration and loss that I did.

Posting my anger on social media would have accomplished nothing. Fearing my home and memories of my mom would be a constant trigger of negativity, I headed to San Diego where my friend and business colleague, Iain, and his wife, Anna—beautiful souls—welcomed me with open arms for six months of healing. I found positivity in writing this book. I planned an upcoming project that honors my mother and disrupts the wellness industry—a change that, had it existed prior to 2017, might have saved her life. Online, I kept myself in a positive place so I could continue to inspire others.

# EFFECTIVE COMMUNICATION

Some people seem to be born with an ease to their interactions with others, but effective communication skills can be learned. Whether you honed your interpersonal skills at a young age or you're still striving, communication skills are vital to your business, inside social media and beyond.

In my early twenties, I worked as an independent contractor for a cable company in Rhode Island. I loved having my own business while going to college. Each day, I chose a neighborhood, mapped out an effi-cient pattern, and knocked door to door. Ask me how many people slammed doors in my face. Let's just say that if I had a quarter for every one, I might be sending spare body parts into space for sport right now. Builds character, as my grandmother used to say.

Nothing teaches you effective communication faster than repeated humiliation. I dug in, shifted my approach a little with each slammed door, the way a research scientist alters one variable in each experi-ment, tweaking my style to get a different outcome. After a while, I averaged eighty dollars per hour in commissions. Time shaped my skills toward a great truth: how I made someone feel was directly proportionate to success. I wasn't selling cable. I was fostering an emotional connection—with me, with the product, with the life they hoped to enjoy by uniting with this company.

Predictive Social Media allows you to have conversation about business with 30 or more new people per day, based on your availabil-ity. Out of the 30 people, maybe you experienced the 1:5 ratio right away, creating 6 new customers or brand advocates. What of the 24 who passed on your business? These 24 people are still valuable. Essential, even. Why let all these people slip through the cracks in your communication?

Now is the time to revolutionize your thinking. These 24 people who passed on your product or service are opportunities to work more diligently at building relationships so that one day, when they have a life experience that brings to mind your product and your friendship, they will enter into business with you.

I'm proud to be able to claim used car salesman as a previous job. No really. Apart from the slick stereotypes of bad fashion and toothy smiles, the job is one of the most challenging in sales. Vehicles are an emotional transaction for most people—not only because of the amount of cash the consumer puts forth, but because so many of life's moments are tied to our cars: bringing babies home from the hospital, driving off to a honeymoon with tin cans tied to the bumper, grown children setting off on their own for the first time.

In my late teens, I shadowed Dan. He was the number one sales rep on the lot. On a particularly slow day during my not-so-epic three-month stint in car sales, Dan said something that I carried with me into every subsequent sales situation.

"The reason I'm number one every month, Jimmy . . ." Jimmy, because, well, Dan was a used car salesman. ". . . isn't because I'm talking to the new people coming onto the lot. I'm number one because I have a constant supply of referrals coming in from happy customers and those people who said no to me in the past but are now ready to buy. I built a relationship with them over time, and it always leads to new business. I constantly have a few thousand people on my list, rotating in and out. That's why you don't see me running out on the lot, trying to grab a new person."

Clearly, time had shaped Dan's truths too. He invested in relationships on the front end so he could find success on the back end. As a former used car salesman, I'm afforded one pun.

The same truth applies to social media.

## COMMUNICATION ACCELERATES FOLLOW UP

Entrepreneurs and business owners don't want to have to keep finding new people with whom to do business. Not only does the acquisition of new potential clients cost more than simply staying in touch, the practice of always chasing new is exhausting. Social media makes maintaining real communication with others easy, and it's a more effective tool than emails, text, app notifications, drum circles, and anything and everything else that exists today, both online and offline.

To those who hold tight the belief that it takes 20 exposures for a customer to act, that's 20 email or text blasts, compared to a few days or weeks using social media. Email, text, and app notifications have their place in business. If these tools are essential to your business, continue them. Just make sure two-way communication through social media remains your primary follow-up strategy. That is how relationships are formed.

Word of mouth sells. **Social media is a two-way movement that allows for follow up and maintaining of customer relationships, over hours, over days, over weeks and months and years.**

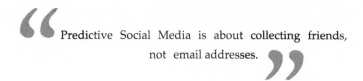

> Predictive Social Media is about collecting friends, not email addresses.

When you post colorful, emotion-driven pictures and videos daily, you give potential prospects more reasons to do business with you, sooner rather than later. Posts and videos that share your personal life build real relationships that convert to business faster. If people request more information about your product or service, social media keeps you off the telephone and out of your car. Platform features offer endless ways to communicate with friends on terms that fit everyone's lifestyle.

Fortune is in the follow up. Days will come when friends have life experiences that open their eyes to your product or service. Staying in touch in the interim via the ongoing communication found in social media is key. When done correctly, follow up is effortless, consistent, and professional. Potential customers rarely fall through the cracks.

Best of all? Social media's response data is unsurpassed—far better than an *opened* or *unopened* email report.

## THE RIGHT BALANCE BETWEEN PERSONAL AND BUSINESS

Social media allows you to post so that friends learn about your personal *and* business life.

How does this help your business?

Remember, people do business with you if they have a real relationship with you. Posting about your personal life allows people to get to know the real you.

**If people know and like the real you, they will look at your business with an open mind. However, in order to win their business, they have to trust you.** In order to trust you, they have to see that you truly believe in what you're selling because you use it yourself.

When posting, add text, pictures, videos, background colors, stickers, and tag others to your post to heighten the emotional bond.

As an added layer of control, some platforms offer an audience selector feature. Audience selector allows you to be private about your personal and business life. You decide who sees which posts.

Alice had a tough upbringing that translated into adult struggles. Marriage and children did not bring her stability. Welfare and thrift stores and charities helped Alice and her family through the darkest times, but no matter how hard she tried, she couldn't get ahead.

One day, someone introduced Alice to the idea of being an entrepreneur. Alice gave it a try. She continued through many challenges, but she had a fire in her soul and a drive to carve out a better future for her children. Over the next few years, Alice turned her life around. Eventually, she became an entrepreneurial success story, turning her small business into a multi-million-dollar empire.

Alice is an exceptional human being with a heart of gold for those who struggle with the same issues she faced before business changed her trajectory. I am proud to call her a friend, and she inspires me with her story. I have witnessed her generosity of spirit and finances and read her posts that brim with enthusiasm and hope. Her intentions are in the right place; however, the majority of her posts relate to her business.

Many times, I have mentioned to her the importance of balance. Just as often, Alice resorts back to business-heavy posts. She is driven to make a difference, so her focus remains on the factor that elevated her from her past—her business. Imagine, however, if she focused on relationships first, business second. Her business would be bigger than it is now—and trust me—it's colossal now.

How do you know if you're like Alice? Please visit your personal profile inside your chosen platform and count how many posts you made over the last two weeks.

Are 80% of the posts about your personal life? No? Then you're like Alice.

Are 20% of the posts about your business life? No? Then you're like Alice.

Are the majority of the people who have liked and commented on these posts already doing business with you in one way or another? If yes, then you're like Alice.

My 80/20 posting guideline has nothing to do with the Pareto Principle mentioned in the first chapter, but it is curious how many business truths seem to revolve around this ratio. Simply stated, 80% of your posts per week should be about your personal life and 20% of your posts per week should be about your business. The 80/20 rule has worked for me for many years.

Remember, people do business with you when they like and trust you, are inspired by you, and have a life experience. People like you if they see you as a friend and have a relationship with you. Friends are nurtured on a personal level. Friendships take time to develop, which is why dedicating the majority of your time to growing these relationships makes good business sense.

Since most people only have a life experience every six months, it makes sense to only spend 20% of your posts on business. Sharing more business posts is not going to speed up someone's life experience. However, more business posts may push friends away. They will think you're all about business and will be turned off by the prospect of building a relationship with you.

## TIMING AND FREQUENCY

Simply applying the 80/20 rule isn't enough. Factors like timing and frequency are equally important.

When possible, I post once in the morning, once in the afternoon, and once around 6 p.m. in my time zone. Some platforms require more posting throughout the day. Sometimes, if a post's likes and comments continue to rise, I'll only post once for the entire day. One time, at four in the morning during a grueling bout of insomnia, I did an inspirational post: a black-and-white selfie and a few heartfelt lines of text. Throughout the day, people liked and commented on that reflective post. By evening, many had sent me private messages to tell me how the post inspired them at the start of their day.

I have posts that receive hundreds of likes and comments, but I take special note of inspiring posts that continues to rise in likes and comments over the course of fifteen hours. A post that generates this much response is a learning opportunity. Clearly, people received a benefit from it. Perhaps it was my honesty, my positivity, my vulnerability. Maybe the light was so awful on the selfie that they thought it was a Calvin Klein ad for a new fragrance called Drowsy, eau de parfum for men.

Generally, I receive more likes and comments on my posts when I post at 9 a.m. in my time zone. If you only do one post a day, this might be the time that works the best for you, as well. Experiment. Try posting in the morning for a week. The next week, post in the afternoon. Try 6 p.m. in your time zone during the third week. Determine the best post times over a few weeks by tracking results. Whichever time gets the most engagement becomes your priority time to make a post every day.

Frequency is also a critical factor to the implementation of the 80/20 guideline. I tend not to post within four hours of my previous post. Why? I notice less likes and comments on my posts when I post more often, and social media works against you when you post with elevated frequency.

As you are posting, social media's algorithms make decisions on what posts friends see based on how they interact on social media. It's not in the best interest of social media to show all posts from one friend at the expense of your other friends' posts. People want to see what all of their friends are doing, not just one friend who dominates social media.

On the flip side, it's also important to post at least once a day because not all friends see your posts all of the time. Social media encourages variety.

If you're comfortable posting once a day already, post twice a day. People check social media at different times during their day. If you only post in the evening and you have 50 friends who only check in the morning, those 50 people may never see your posts. The maximum amount of posts per day should be three on most social media platforms. Surpassing three makes it difficult to stay aligned with the four-hour frequency suggestion I gave you. Consistency is key. Remain relevant and visible because friends will have a life experience, and you need to be ready.

## VIEWING

Most platforms offer custom preferences that allow you to decide which posts you see from friends.

Prioritizing preferences allows you to choose whose posts you always want to see when you check in on social media. How is that for never missing a post from someone you care about most? Never miss a post from one of your most important friends, customers, or brand advocates. Talk about building a quick, strong relationship!

Social media uses sophisticated algorithms that do a good job of showing you posts from friends that may be of interest to you. Platforms don't share how they do this, but they do give us an idea. The offerings are based on how you interact on social media. Liking and commenting—even pausing your scroll on certain images and ads and videos—and being a member of a community or business page are all factors in this algorithm. It works. You'll spend your precious time communicating with people on social media who are the most important to you and your business.

For the curious among you, a quick online search will give you a more technical breakdown of these algorithms. Experts abound and each platform is different. Applied correctly, Predictive Social Media works, regardless of algorithms.

If your preferred platform allows you to browse most recent posts from friends, you'll feel in-the-know but you may have to sort through less interesting posts from friends. Not everyone posts great content all the time. Even the most interesting man in the world might slip and post about his cat's hair ball before he's had his morning coffee.

Tinker between favorite and recent features to see which works the best for you.

## LINKS

Inserting links into posts encourages people to click whatever content you deem important. Posting links is a one-way, outbound train ticket. People who follow the link are not likely to reverse tracks simply to like or comment. Without likes or comments, you cannot be sure friends are looking at your posts. Likes and comments give you a prime opportunity to continue communication. How can you build a relationship with friends when your links encourage the train to leave the station?

## LINKS IN PERSONAL POSTS

Instead of inserting a link to an article or source you believe is great content, become familiar with the article or source, mine important pieces, and reflect on them inside a post. Encourage communication about the subject inside the comment section of your post instead of driving friends to another website.

Let's say I read an article about entrepreneurship that really resonated with me. Instead of posting a link to the article and sending my friends away to read the article, I took out pieces that were important to me and shared my thoughts about those pieces—what I learned and how it related to my life. It's no different than meeting a friend for coffee and saying, "Hey, I read this great tip about how to get the best airline deals." You'd never tell your friend, "You should pick up the same magazine and read all about it." You'd give them the tip, right then and there, then expound on how this nugget of information relates to your life. In turn, your friend would likely offer feedback from his or her life related to the same topic.

Social media is no different.

## LINKS IN BUSINESS POSTS

Instead of inserting a link that sends friends to your website or a landing page to give them more information about your business, why not choose one thing about your business that's important to you and post about it? Let friends like and comment. Then take the communication private with each friend through social media. People are more likely to do business with you when you communicate directly with them. Driving them to a website discourages active communication. Links in business posts send friends away with a one-way ticket to Make-Your-Own-Decision Land, a place where you neither reside nor visit. Stay active in the process. Encourage friends to stay and like or comment.

People love original content. It shows intent and thoughtfulness, not simply a reflex action while you're waiting in line for your sub sandwich at lunch. Social media loves original content, too, and pushes organic posts out more frequently than posts shared from someone else. When social media loves something, it is seen more. When people love something, likes and comments multiply.

If you find someone else's post inspiring and you want to share it, post it as fresh content and give credit to the person who originally posted. Many times, at the bottom of my posts, I tag a person's name to give him or her credit for the content. I might use someone's picture and add my own caption. Then, below my new caption, I write: *@Marianne – I had to re-share your picture. Thanks for posting it!* Do not lift content without proper credit.

## THE 30-DAY RESET BUTTON

My friend Jason is a family man. He never decides without first considering how the choice impacts his family. When I met Jason, he was posting more than 20% per week about business. Like everyone else, he did it for the right reasons. He did it for his family. He thought if he stayed in front of people about his business, they would become his customer in a shorter period of time.

After a consult, he made a commitment to me. Under no circumstance would he post more than 20% a week about his business. I asked him to spend the next 30 days *only* talking about his personal life since all of his friends were used to him talking about business all the time.

"Think of it as a reset button," I said.

He agreed.

After 30 days, Jason noticed a lot of his social media friends who had not communicated with him much in the past conversed with him a great deal more. This reset, alone, made him fall in love with the system. He told me that even if his business did not grow, he was thankful that he was developing real friendships. Jason focused on the 80/20 rule for the 30 days following this reset period. Forty-five days later, Jason and 10 of his brand advocates had captured over 60 new customers for his business. Jason was ecstatic. He had never seen this type of growth before in such a short period of time.

Are you like Jason when I first met him? Don't be afraid to do a reset. Without the personal relationship component, your business will struggle. Using this process will move your business faster than you ever thought possible. Hitting the reset button for 30 days may feel, at first, like treading backwards. In reality, you'll be taking a giant leap forward.

# EFFECTIVE BUSINESS POSTS (THE 20%)

Business posts focus on facts, emotions, or a combination of both. **The most effective business post is about what has happened in your life involving the business during the previous week.** These business testimonials originate from the heart and tap into your emotions, which, in turn, tap into your friends' emotions. Here, we'll explore four types of business social media posts across all different categories and industries of business.

The following examples represent categories of business across a variety of industries and are for instructive purposes only. Insert your words, your voice, your personality, or your posts will not be uniquely you. As with all posts, be sure to include relevant photos or videos to increase engagement.

## PERSONAL BUSINESS POSTS

A personal business post is anything that is personal to you *about* your business. The post can discuss something from last week or years earlier. Often, they involve the motivation behind your chosen business.

**Brand Advocate** (Sells wellness products): *I was thinking about how people use the words health and wellness as if they mean the same thing. I was once told that health is about people being sick and taking medication while wellness is about the natural ways of staying healthy and not getting sick in the first place. What are your thoughts?*

**Independent Contractor** (Realtor): *I was so excited to help Christel and Darren purchase their home. They had been searching for six months. It feels great to play a small part in helping to build a family's memories.*

**Small Business** (Chiropractor): *I hired Sandra. She's excited to get started and learn as much as possible about running a chiropractic office. I can't wait for all of you to meet her.*

**Brand** (Famous dentist who does seminars around the country): *This morning I was thinking about how many people don't floss daily. It only takes a few minutes and prevents problems down the road. Just saying.*

**Company** (Established company): *My partner and I were thinking this morning about how we started this company with two people. Today, we employ 150 people around the world and have helped 10,000 families live a better life. Chase your dreams. Never give up.*

Remember to talk from your heart, as if you're speaking to a good friend. The more conversational, the more emotion the post will contain, and the more likes and comments you will get. The moment you sound like you're selling something is the moment you kiss your likes and comments goodbye.

Add text and images to these 20% business posts when possible. Another option is to post a video of you talking. If you're out in a public place, use a check-in feature on your post. Often, I'll add emoticons to inject how I am feeling. A wide range of cartoon faces offers a fast and friendly shortcut to my emotions at the time of the post. Remember to gravitate to the positive side of emoticons.

If you post once a day and follow the 80/20 rule, this post will take care of one of the two business posts you should be doing per week. One post per day equals seven posts a week. Twenty percent is, roughly, two business posts a week.

### WEEKLY UPDATE POSTS

These posts cover anything you wish to discuss regarding your business over the past seven days. Although friends may not be customers now, they'll witness your passion or wonderment or any other positive emotion you wish to share right along with your update and feel inspired.

Here are examples. Be sure to use words unique to you and post applicable photos or videos.

**Brand Advocate** (Sells wellness products): *I started my weight loss program two weeks ago. Already, I'm back to the size of my favorite jeans! I couldn't be prouder. I'm feeling inspired every day. Way to go, me!*

**Independent Contractor** (Realtor): *I love doing walk-throughs on houses. I did four this week for my real estate business. It always amazes me how the architecture changes in every house.*

**Small Business** (Chiropractor): *I've run a successful chiropractor clinic for 12 years. We're taking our business to a new level of service by adding massage. As a gift to my social media friends, come in and receive a 50% discount off massage for the next two weeks. Tell the front desk "Social media sent me" to receive the discount.*

**Brand** (Famous dentist who does seminars around the country): *This past week, I met a dentist from Texas during one of my seminars. He shared his struggles with getting more people through the door. It's only been six days since that chat, and he's already seen an increase from just one of my tips. Sometimes, it's the simple things that make all the difference. Thanks for connecting with me, Joe.*

**Company** (Established company): *This past week, we acquired our 10,000th customer! We can't tell you how good we feel knowing we're changing lives every day. Thank you to everyone who helped make this happen!*

## EDUCATIONAL POSTS

Educational Posts are your opportunity to be a teacher. Make a list of everything you can talk about as it pertains to your business. Go as far as listing every ingredient in your product. This is your opportunity to talk facts regarding your business while using emotion. This is where friends witness passion coming from you as you discuss hot topics. This is where you build trust, thus becoming an inspiration to friends about the type of products and services you market.

Below, find example posts with an educational perspective. Again, change the words so they reflect you. Adding relevant photos or videos will make them shine.

**Brand Advocate** (Sells wellness products): *Weight loss can be tricky. Have you heard of the ingredient ____ ? It's known to curb your appetite.*

**Independent Contractor** (Realtor): *When buying a home, here are the top three things to consider.*

**Small Business** (Chiropractor): *The number one reason someone visits a chiropractor is _____.*

**Brand** (Famous dentist who does seminars around the country): *The number one reason someone visits a dentist is _____.*

**Company** (Established company): *Not everyone knows the different kinds of metal and their quality when purchasing jewelry. Our jewelry company has been in business 18 years. Here's a quick guide to being an informed buyer.*

### ASK YOUR FRIENDS POST

Try a post where you ask your friends directly if they would have an interest in your business. Limit these posts to once a month. Be sure to include a picture or video of you with the product.

Some examples:

**Brand Advocate** (Sells wellness products): *Would anyone have interest in receiving a sample? I've lost 19 pounds using this product so far, and many more people are seeing even better results.*

**Independent Contractor** (Realtor): *I've been a realtor for 15 years. I've helped hundreds of people buy and sell homes, and I'm pretty passionate about it. If you happen to know anyone in that transitional time of their lives who needs help, I would love the opportunity.*

**Small Business** (Chiropractor): *I've owned my chiropractic practice for eight years, and I still enjoy meeting new people as they walk in the door. They come in with pain and leave with a smile. If you're curious about how chiropractic services can help you, let me know. First-time discounts to those who come in because of social media.*

**Brand** (Famous dentist who does seminars around the country): *I've been a dentist for 20 years before I started doing seminars around the world, helping other dentists build thriving practices. If you're curious how I can help your dental practice, please let me know.*

**Company** (Established company): *Would anyone have an interest in checking out some beautiful jewelry? We have been in business for 18 years and are offering a friends' discount to all our social media friends this week.*

Personal Business, Weekly, Educational, and Ask Your Friends posts are all effective variations of business posts. Cycle these posts throughout the week. If you post once a day, then business posts should be two posts per week (based on the 20% guideline). Over the course of one month, this adds up to eight business posts.

Eight business posts per month means:

**1** Personal Business Post a Week  **=4** Business Posts a Month

**2** Weekly Update Business Posts a Month **=2** Business Posts a Month
(Every Other Week)

**1** Educational Business Post Per Month

**1** Ask Your Friends Business Post Per Month

## RESPONDING TO LIKES OR COMMENTS ON BUSINESS POSTS

Wait 48 hours from the time you posted to reply. Your post may linger around, and you'll notice that you continue to collect likes and comments days later. Some businesspeople reply almost in real time, but this sends the wrong message. If you're building a successful business, you should not have so much time on your hands that you check your posts constantly throughout the day.

- Reply publicly to each comment on your post so everyone sees your interaction with that person.
- If you've spoken to the commenter about your business less than 90 days ago, *do not* send a private message. Close out the message box and go to the next profile. Why? Because if you're constantly reaching out to friends and asking them to look at your business, they will stop liking or commenting on your business post. Keep in mind that most people have a life experience every six months.

- If it has been more than 90 days since the last time you spoke to that commenter about your business, send a private message. Try, *Hey* (friend)*! I noticed you commented on my post a couple of days ago about _____ . It's been a few months since I've spoken to you about my business. Things are going well.* (In the next 1-2 sentences give an update of your business since the last time you spoke to your friend.) *Would you have an interest in checking it out? If not, as always, I really appreciate our friendship.*
- If the person responds with no interest, reply, *No problem. I hope you're doing well. Looking forward to staying in touch.*
- If the person responds with interest, this person will enter into the part of the system called Conversation. Recall that when people express interest, you add them to your customer community. If they are already in the community, message them the link so they can revisit and check out the announcement post.
- Repeat the same steps with those who liked the post.

## EFFECTIVE PERSONAL POSTS (THE 80%)

Before social media, it was common for someone to grieve by them-selves or with a few close friends. I allowed my social media friends into my grief by posting a special photo of my grandmother.

I remember the day well. Strange, because it was so ordinary at the time. My grandmother sat in a chair by her favorite bay window, enjoying her morning coffee with other family members assembled around the kitchen table. I knelt next to her so that we were eye to eye, smile to smile. Across the table, my mom snapped a photo. The photo was memorable because we weren't posing for the camera. We barely knew the moment had been captured. It was simply one of a million other ordinary moments that conveyed a love that outdistances words.

In addition to the photo, I posted a paragraph of my feelings—what she meant to me, words of wisdom she shared, how she made me laugh every single time I was with her. I let my friends into an emotionally vulnerable space at a time when I needed to feel supported. Within a few days, 357 social media friends had either liked or commented on the post. In fact, 110 of 357 left a comment to share words of support and love. Many sent me private messages to express their condolences. The closeness I felt with my social media friends aided my healing and cemented relationships.

On many occasions since, I've had social media friends mention that post about my grandmother because it made an impact in their lives. Perhaps they went home that night and called their grandmothers, simply because they could. Perhaps it gave them reassurance that the bonds we make in this life don't end with the passing of a loved one. Perhaps my positivity in the face of adversity gave them hope in their personal trials.

The post about my grandmother is considered a personal post. It's what I want you to do 80% of the time when you post. Share what holds meaning for you—deaths, births, events that make you smile, something your child did that frazzled you, a small gesture your husband does to light up your day. Share random thoughts you have as you're walking down the road and notice the wind against your cheeks. Share weddings and parties and joy. It's not about whether or not you have an exciting or dull life. **We all have exciting lives when we value what's right in front of us. Let friends know what is right in front of you. That is how relationships take root and grow.**

It's important to share a variety of aspects of your life. It's common for a mother to post a lot about her children. It's common for a single guy to post about all the parties he attends. It's common for an entrepreneur or businessperson to only post about business-related experiences. Isn't there more to you? If you only show one side of you, that is the only thing you will be known for. The best relationships are built when you show all aspects of your life to others.

If you're a mother with children, you may also like to write poems in your spare time. Share those with friends on social media. If you're a single guy, you also might be into cars. Show off your favorite cars to friends on social media. You might think you're all business, but you also might like to hike. Take pictures along the path of your favorite trail.

How do you write a great personal post? Lead with your emotions. Open your heart. Be honest, genuine, transparent. Remember those moments when you let down your guard. Think of a time you cried and let it all out, or a moment you laughed so hard you struggled to draw breath. Each time you write a post, strive for beautiful emotions.

Appendix B offers additional inspiration for personal posts. Here are examples of my personal posts over a two-week period.

*Found this picture from 18 years ago. Wow! Do you see me?* (Image: My friends and I at a nightclub when I was 22 years old)

*I love beautiful environments.* (Image: Marianne and I sitting in front of a water fountain in Sedona)

*Love being silly with her.* (Image: Marianne standing beneath a giant iron horse)

*A boy amongst giants is how I describe Mason's 1st year in T-ball. At 3 yrs. old, he played with 5-yr-olds. He would hit the ball and chase it instead of running to 1st base, run the bases instead of waiting for his teammate to hit the ball, or chase a butterfly while standing out in the field. He did his thing, and we love it.* (Image: end of season team baseball picture)

*Family first. Miss you, Nana. My grandmother passed in 2013. Always think about her. She's sitting in this picture.* (Image: my grandmother and family at a family picnic 20 years ago)

*It's 4:30 AM. I think what drives us is our values. These values give us a greater purpose on Earth than our own needs. It seems the only way to really be the bosses of our own lives.* (Image: me writing my values on a whiteboard)

*I'm still wondering why I had a boxing session with this cactus on my hike. Sometimes, I do the weirdest things.* (Image: I am boxing a cactus)

*Mason puts this puzzle together effortlessly, all by himself. It amazes me what he can do for just turning 3 years old.* (Image: Mason on the floor putting together a puzzle)

*Some pictures soften my heart. This is one. Mason and Nana spending time together at Disney.* (Image: I found a picture from a couple of years ago and wanted to re-share it on social media)

*If you could pull anything out of this blue cup, what would it be?* (Image: I am sitting at a coffee shop holding a blue cup)

## RESPONDING TO LIKES OR COMMENTS ON PERSONAL POSTS

Similar to business posts, wait 48 hours to respond to your personal posts. Follow the same steps you did with your business posts. If your last conversation with the person was less than 90 days ago, do not respond. If your last conversation with the person was more than 90 days ago, feel free to send a private message.

*Hey* (friend)*! I noticed you commented on my post a couple of days ago about _____ . It's been a few months since I've spoken to you. Just wanted to say hi!*

Repeat the same steps with those who liked the post.

## RESPONDING TO FRIENDS' POSTS AND STORIES

Like a friend's post or story when you don't have anything worthy to say or your response is strictly an emotion that you feel. Consider adding emoticons based on the emotion you want to portray.

Personally, I like to pull out my phone and scroll through my friends' posts throughout the day. It's easy to find a minute here and there to do this activity. No sooner do I like a post than I see that same person liking or commenting on one of my posts. It sure beats the days that I had to call everyone on the phone to have the same type of communication.

Comment on friends' posts or reply to stories when you have something to say. Talk from the heart and be yourself. You will gain new friends from those who are reading the comments on your friends' posts. Another form of connection.

Most of my comments are less than five words long. You don't have to write a novel to create meaning; you simply need to speak from your heart. Use stickers in place of words. For example, I might write, *I really love this post. Thank you for sharing.* Or I use the sticker of a giant smiley face where the eyes are replaced with hearts. More often than not, I tend to use the smiley face in place of words. Me, attempting to be more emotional.

## SOCIAL MEDIA, LIVE

Live broadcasts are a special feature of some platforms. I once did a live session in the kitchen of an Airbnb that I rented in Scottsdale, Arizona. I wanted the feel of friends gathered around a table, looking out at the breathtaking and memorable desert vista.

To best prepare for the session, I planned ahead. Two weeks prior, I chatted up the session to build excitement. In one post, I asked social media friends what they would like to learn. In another post, I asked how they already used certain features on social media. In all the buzz posts leading up to the live session, I stoked the conversation in the comment sections.

When the session started, many people waited with anticipation. I welcomed everyone, asked where they were from—which prompted additional conversations based on what I knew of their area—and chatted as new friends to give everyone time to log on. When a reasonable amount of introductory time had passed, I launched into my social media training, the topic I most wanted to cover during the session. As I spoke, I watched people's comments and questions scroll. I answered questions in real time, which left participants with the sense that they were heard and valued, despite not being seen on video. People came and went throughout the hour-long session. Hundreds of comments later, the session ended with everyone pumped.

The story above would fall under the 20% business post category. Create live sessions for the 80% personal posts as well.

It's about being able to share what's on your mind. If you want to interact with friends in real time, live is the best route to go. From a business perspective, you help potential customers and customers get their questions answered and get feedback from them on how to better your business. Live features work well because people love watching video. Those who want to follow your live sessions receive notifications when you go live so they know to tune in.

Make sure you have a strong Wi-Fi or roaming signal. If you want to use a cell phone for live events, be sure to keep your plan updated and look for unlimited data and improved connections. If the signal is too weak, your live session will be a waste of time.

Plan your live session for the greatest impact.

- Choose your audience. Control who sees your live session. Often, you can allow friends only, certain friends, or a friend list, or open your session to anyone by choosing the public option.
- Select your audience based upon your goals for the session. With existing customers, discuss something new that is happening with your product or service. If you want to make an announcement regarding your business and you want everyone to be able to access it, choose the public option.
- Write a captivating description that represents your live session. This gives viewers a sneak peek into the session's content.

Once you go live:

- People will log on as they see the session pop up. Ask viewers to follow your live videos so they get notifications next time you go live.
- Add filters, doodles, or masks to make your video fun. Mention names of viewers as they come onto the session. Everyone enjoys being recognized and welcomed.
- Many platforms save the event on your timeline once the session is complete, similar to a recorded video, so people can watch it at a time convenient to them. Additionally, some platforms offer the option to download the session to the camera roll on your phone or delete the session entirely.

Use live features to broadcast breaking news about your business, interview someone who brings credibility to your business, demonstrate your product, answer questions from those who care about your business, or showcase behind-the-scenes information about your business.

Live sessions are a great tool to explore hot topics that get people excited about your business and an excellent way to create instant communication with friends. Use this feature when you want friends to see where you are or when you want them to talk to you in real time and believe such conversations will benefit a greater group. While in a live session, encourage friends to invite others to join the session.

## PREDICTIVE CHECKLIST: COMMUNICATION

❒ Posting is about giving friends a sneak peek into your personal and business life. Apply the 80/20 rule because friends care more about you than your business.

❒ Posting at different times throughout the day will get you different levels of engagement.

❒ Obey the four-hour rule. Post fresh content 1-3 times a day.

❒ Avoid linking and sharing the posts of others. Instead, share your thoughts about the content while giving proper credit to the source.

❒ Responding to friends' posts shows them you care about their lives.

❒ Like friends' posts when you don't have anything substantial to say; comment with something meaningful so you are part of the communication between your friends and their friends.

---

*Looking ahead:* **Business can't just be about selling a product or service; business *shouldn't* be about selling a product or service.** Before you dismiss me as a dreamer and an idealist whose feet never touch the ground, read what comes next. The world of business is changing. Predictive Social Media has the power to disrupt it all—independent contractor to global corporation.

# CHAPTER ELEVEN

## You, Me, We—Together

"*Never chase the next hot thing. Stop trying to chase the wave. You will never catch it. You always for the most part find out about that stuff too late. Instead, do what you are really passionate about, what you really love. That will position you before the wave even hits, and you will find out about whatever it is before the wave starts, before it gets hot, and that is how you take advantage.*" ~Elon Musk

ELON'S WORDS resonate with me. I never immersed myself in this space for money. I never did it to chase the next wave. I am passionate about social media—specifically, how to scale relationships and inspire friends of businesses—brand advocates—to share products and services with other friends on a variety of platforms.

My friends, you're in a desirable position. No matter if you've spent the past few years marketing your business through social platforms to modest success or if you're approaching social media and its word-of-mouth capacity with fresh and hungry eyes, you are at the cusp of a rip tide in business. Traditional methods of reaching customers will carry dated businesses out to sea.

**Those who embrace and flourish inside of social media will build success that is resistant to subsequent storms.**

Relationship bonds between people who are passionate about your product or service are an equal force of nature.

The passion found in Predictive Social Media—yours, mine, ours—positions us before the wave. In a boat. *Together.*

Now.

Early readers and those who climb aboard all the system has to offer will conquer *your* market. It's inevitable. Take an honest assessment of your business past, your current business. Relationships work. They've *always* worked. You know this because you feel its goodness and truth, intuitively, every day.

Now, relationships are online. Social media is a continuation of what you've always done to be successful in business. Now, relationships are measurable and efficient and flexible and achievable.

For the first time in business history, it's possible to *prove* that word of mouth, through social media relationships, scales.

As word gets around that you and I—we, *together*—have united the strength of social media word of mouth with a proven mathematical formula that guarantees results, businesses of all categories and sizes will reel from the success the system brings. Competitors will blend and dilute the front-wave moment.

Whether you want your product or service to dominate your street, Main Street, city streets, or the internet superhighway, businesses of all sizes and uniqueness who have the ability to predict social media will achieve what others simply cannot.

Predictive Social Media doesn't work with the toes-dipped-in approach. Seven components, all working in harmony, produce monumental results. Hesitating or dabbling, just for a bit, to see what happens, is a surefire way for your business to be carried out to sea.

Your competitors are already embracing the power of social media. At the macro level, Fortune 500 companies are tripping over themselves to grab hold, measure, and predict the passion that people have for their products and services, worldwide. And that *other* store across town? Your primary micro-level competitor? You can bet they're bringing someone on board their team right now whose sole job is to grow those online word-of-mouth relationships on behalf of their business.

When Six Sigma launched thirty years ago, mainstream business believed the idea that an organizational process, applied to everything from quality control to employee morale, with a guaranteed output was absurd—so far outside the box at that time as to be perceived as pure fantasy. Thirty years later, along with nearly every mega-global enterprise today, the Walt Disney Corporation enjoys the fruits of that fantasy—inside their products and inside the boardroom. Brands like Nike, General Mills, Calvin Klein, and innumerable other household name-companies are launching brand advocate programs, *now*, attempting to capture and monetize online relationships.

**In your hands, through your reader or listening device—now is *your* moment for *your* business. Endorsed by Six Sigma and powered by everyday extraordinary businesspeople like you, me, us, this journey we are on together will be unprecedented.**

Get in touch with me on your favorite social media site. You'll find me there. Connect with me, personally. Send me a private message. Tell me how this book has made a difference in your life. Tell me how Predictive Social Media has grown your business. No matter if you are a one-person operation in the UK or the largest company in Asia, no matter your industry, I want to be part of your social media journey. Be sure to take advantage of **free** resources at **jimlupkin.com** to help you implement the system in your business.

I'm an entrepreneur, just like you, who believes that a rising tide floats all boats. I believe social media is a tremendous force for good in this world, if only we honor that responsibility to each other in the right way. I believe in the ability of relationships to bring people out of dark corners of loss and hopelessness into light, and I believe that sustainable, certain, measurable systems bring peace and clarity to the sometimes-frightening world of business.

And I happen to believe that my social media system is predictive of success.

Your success.

I believe in you, and I believe in us, *together*.

Let's do this.

ENJOY THIS BOOK? YOU CAN MAKE A BIG DIFFERENCE.

Honest reviews of this book help bring the attention of new readers who will benefit from the Predictable Social Media system. If you enjoyed this book, I would be grateful for a few minutes of your time to visit your preferred online book retailer or online book review site to spread the love.

Thank you,

# Acknowledgments

To God (or whatever name you associate with the force that connects us), thank you for giving me the inner drive to help others realize their full potential. You've allowed me to do this as a leader, a visionary, and a cheerleader and instilled in me the belief that giving of myself is more valuable than taking.

Mom, thank you for being my biggest cheerleader and my brightest light in life. Your ability to tell stories and connect with others passed down to me and is evident in this book. I love you.

Dad, thank you for inspiring me throughout the years. Your ability to think systematically and your no-nonsense approach to getting things done contributes to my success. I love you.

Nanny, thank you for encouraging me to express myself honestly. This book would not be the same without that self-expression. I love you.

To my wife, Marianne, thank you for showing me the emotional side of life. With an increased emotional intelligence comes a heart-centered approach to this book. I love you.

To my children, Jade, Mason and Jessalyn, thank you for filling my life with smiles, laughter, joy, reminders of what's essential in life, and the inspiration to better myself every day. I love you.

To L.A. Mitchell, thank you for helping me create this masterpiece of a book. Your ability to move people through words astounds me.

To Maria Kelsey-Palmer, thank you for the visuals found throughout this book. Each creation shows your passion for the system, your love of teaching, and your genuine heart.

To the Jim Lupkin brand team—Iain Bratt, L.A. Mitchell, Ben Berry, Gillian Murray, Denver Nowicz, Tracy Hamilton, and Maria Kelsey-Palmer—thank you for your countless hours and commitment. Your relentless pursuit to share the teachings found in this book is inspiring.

Jay Anderson, thank you for sharing your inspirational story so that others may find light in their darkest moments using social media. Your story will undoubtedly inspire others.

Donna Marie Serritella, thank you for sharing your compliance knowledge in the book. Your contribution will help many businesses take a preventative approach and avoid costly mistakes.

To my business colleagues and social media friends, thank you for sharing your life and for being part of mine. Each experience has made me a better person.

Lastly, to my beta readers—Lonnie Mckinney, Donna Marie Serritella, Jay Anderson, Tracy Hamilton, Doug Firebaugh, Tara Williams, Nicole Bowles, David Dillingham, Troy Dooly, Kim Thompson Pinder, Iain Bratt, Maria Kelsey-Palmer, Ben Berry, and Gillian Murray—thank you for taking the time to provide invaluable feedback to ensure the book delivers on its promise.

| | | | |
|---|---|---|---|
| Authenticity | Equality | Love | Simplicity |
| Acceptance | Exploration | Loyalty | Spirituality |
| Achievement | Fairness | Mastery | Stability |
| Adaptability | Faith | Maturity | Success |
| Adventure | Fame | Meaning | Status |
| Altruism | Family | Moderation | Stewardship |
| Amusement | Focus | Openness | Strength |
| Attentiveness | Freedom | Optimism | Structure |
| Authority | Friendships | Originality | Support |
| Autonomy | Fun | Passion | Tolerance |
| Balance | Generosity | Patience | Tranquility |
| Beauty | Grace | Peace | Transparency |
| Boldness | Gratitude | Pleasure | Trustworthiness |
| Bravery | Growth | Playfulness | Truth |
| Candor | Happiness | Poise | Uniqueness |
| Challenge | Harmony | Popularity | Unity |
| Charity | Health | Purpose | Valor |
| Citizenship | Honesty | Quality | Vison |
| Community | Honor | Recognition | Wealth |
| Compassion | Hope | Recreation | Wisdom |
| Competency | Humor | Religion | Wonder |
| Contribution | Imagination | Reputation | |
| Consistency | Independence | Respect | |
| Courage | Influence | Responsibility | |
| Creativity | Inner | Restraint | |
| Curiosity | Integrity | Reverence | |
| Dedication | Intelligence | Risk | |
| Dependability | Joy | Security | |
| Determination | Justice | Self-reliance | |
| Development | Kindness | Self-respect | |
| Discovery | Knowledge | Sensitivity | |
| Empathy | Leadership | Serenity | |
| Energy | Learning | Service | |
| | Liberty | Silence | |

# Appendix B

## IDEAS FOR PERSONAL POSTS (THE 80%)

- Write a post about the light coming through your window. Be present, in the moment, and invite friends into that moment.
- Start with "I remember…" Your memory might be five hours ago or five years ago. Tie it back to your core values.
- Choose a color and take a 15-minute walk. Notice instances of that color. Take photos. Share what you found.
- Visualize a place you really love. Write a post about it. Give sensory details. Invite friends to share their favorite place.
- Write about the streets of your city.
- Write about reading and books that changed your life.
- Open a poetry book to any page, grab a line, and continue the thought from there.
- Set a timer for three minutes. List your obsessions. This will show you how you consciously and subconsciously spend your waking, thoughtful hours. Find the positives about these obsessions and write about them. Friends love to discover your passions.
- Motivational speaker Jim Rohn is quoted as saying, "You're the average of the five people you spend the most time with." Write about someone you admire that you'd like to

add as one of your five. Aim for authentic, real people, not celebrities.

- You're planning a virtual business dinner. Write about who would get an invitation and why. What would be on the menu?
- If you had access to a time machine and could live the day over, what would you have done differently?
- Write and post a review of books you love, business or otherwise. Be sure to copy and paste them to your favorite online store. Like social proof with Jim's system, authors depend on those reviews for sales.
- If you can't think of anything to post, write about a meal you once had. Everyone loves food.
- Some days, the struggle and internal resistance is real. Instead, today, view your post as a mini vacation from life.
- If you struggle with all the eyes that will read your post, write to one ideal reader.

More Ideas:

Keep a journal/list of ideas for posts. When it's time to write one, you'll always have material.

Start a file on your laptop or save photos in a special file in your phone. When you have thirty free minutes, browse free photography sites for images that move you, that inspire you to say something.

---
---
---
---
---
---
---
---
---
---
---
---
---

# Appendix C

## QUICK GUIDE FOR BUSINESS POSTS (THE 20%)

- Talk from the heart. Business posts with emotion generate more likes and comments.
- Add relevant images to all posts.
- Consider posting a video of you speaking.
- Emojis and emoticons boost the emotion inside text.

**1 Personal Business Post a week = 4 business posts a month.**

- Anything that is personal to you *about* your business.
- The post can discuss something from last week or years earlier.
- Often involves the motivation behind your chosen business.

**2 Weekly Update Business Posts a month (every other week) = 2 business posts a month.**

- Anything you wish to discuss regarding your business over the past seven days.
- Allow friends to witness your passion about your product or service.

**1 Educational Business Post per month.**

- Make a list of everything you can talk about as it pertains to your business.
- Discuss ingredients.
- Facts about your business + passion.
- This is where you build trust and become an inspiration to friends about the type of products and services you market.

**1 Ask Your Friends Business Post per month.**

- Ask your friends directly if they would have an interest in your business.
- Limit these kinds of posts to once a month.
- Be sure to include a picture or video of you with the product.

1. Tankovska, H. "Daily Social Media Usage Worldwide." Statista, February 8, 2021. https://www.statista.com/statistics/433871/daily-social-media-usage-worldwide/.

2. Disruptive Strategy (Clayton Christensen), "Disruptive Innovation," Harvard Business Online, video accessed March 11, 2021, private URL.

3. Albrecht, Karl. "The (Only) 5 Fears We All Share." Psychology Today. Sussex Publishers, March 22, 2012.

4. Tsaousides, Theo. "Why Are We Scared of Public Speaking?" Psychology Today. Sussex Publishers, November 27, 2017. https://www.psychologytoday.com/us/blog/smashing-the-brainblocks/201711/why-are-we-scared-public-speaking. Accessed March 21, 2021.

5. "Research Overview." Direct Selling Association, 2019. https://www.dsa.org/statistics-insights/overview.

6. "Advertising FAQ's: A Guide for Small Business." Federal Trade Commission, January 15, 2021. https://www.ftc.gov/tips-advice/business-center/guidance/advertising-faqs-guide-small-business.

7. Edunov, By: Sergey, Smriti Bhagat, Moira Burke, Carlos Diuk, and Ismail Onur Filiz. "Three and a Half Degrees of Separation." Facebook Research, March 1, 2021. https://research.fb.com/blog/2016/02/three-and-a-half-degrees-of-separation/.

# ABOUT THE AUTHOR

As one of the world's foremost social media architects, Jim Lupkin helps businesses build a framework capable of withstanding the turbulent and ever-changing social media climate. From a $6 billion global corporation to celebrity style brands to small businesses, solopreneurs, and brand advocates in more than 100 countries, his passion lies at the intersection between the entrepreneurial spirit and the magic that happens when people work in harmony toward a common goal.

His core value, *enlighten,* led him to study the true nature of disruptive innovation as a recent graduate of Harvard Business School online and Babson college online. A three-time author and international speaker, Jim aims to turn his proven social media system toward a much-needed disruption in the world of business.

He lives with his wife, Marianne, and their two children in Pennsylvania.

# LEAVE A LEGACY THAT LASTS A LIFETIME.

For more information about how you can be a live donor
or to register to donate your organs posthumously, visit
organdonor.gov (US)
or the International Registry on Organ Donation and Transplantation
at
irodat.org

# DIRECTSELLINGSOLUTIONS.COM

Donna Marie Serritella and her team have provided field compliance services to direct selling companies worldwide since 1991.

Donna Marie, known as the Queen of Compliance, may be reached through her company's site, www.DirectSellingSolutions.com

Made in the USA
Las Vegas, NV
25 September 2023

78118747R00129